A HOUSE NOT MADE
WITH HANDS

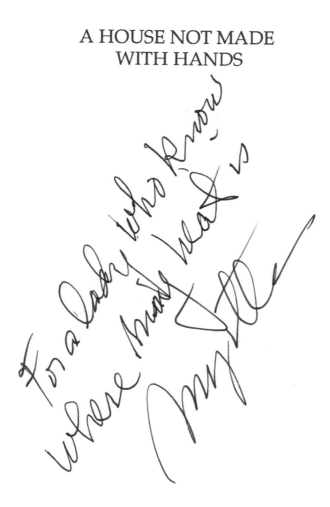

A HOUSE NOT MADE WITH HANDS

MYRTLE STEDMAN

Sunstone Press
Santa Fe, New Mexico

Library of Congress Cataloging in Publication Data

Stedman, Myrtle.
        A house not made with hands / Myrtle Stedman. -- 1st ed.
                p.   cm.
        ISBN 0-86534-145-1 : $12.95
        1. Stedman, Myrtle. 2. Architects -- New Mexico -- Biography.
I. Title.
NA737.S637A2 1990
720' .92--dc20
[B]   90-9999
                                                                    CIP

Published in 1990 by SUNSTONE PRESS
        Post Office Box 2321
        Santa Fe, New Mexico 87504-2321 USA

Dedicated to

Marion and Edith

We are shaped and fashioned
by what we love.

—RAINER MARIA RILKE

"I can see you as a robin."
"When I live again,
I would like to be one."

That dried-up robin came up out of its shallow grave, shook the loose dirt from his feathers, walked around the corner of the studio and back onto the flagstone on the portal, looked for a moment at the place beneath the studio window where he had lain all winter, then turned and walked the full length of the portal, talking to me in chirps.

At my feet, he turned onto the flagstone walk, stopped a second to pluck at a piece of dried grass.

I saw that his bill was still bent from smashing into the glass.

And it struck me that he was walking on a flagstone walk that I'd put down after Sted's death, as though it were familiar.

CHAPTER 1

On four separate occasions my mother had asked, "Do you think you want to marry this man?"

With the first one, I said, "I don't know." The second, "No." The third, "Bah!"

And the fourth time, "Yes, I guess I must, because when he holds me close to him and kisses me, I feel an irresistible urge. And I think that if he should really love me, I'd be like a black widow spider and devour him before he could get away."

"My stars! You say the craziest things. I never will understand you, never. Here I was, thinking you were the most innocent child ever, and you talk like a, like a...oh, never mind. I don't know what's the matter that I should have such children," she continued. "I wish I'd died before I met your father."

"Oh, Mama, if I were to say it in a nice way, I'd say that he and I could get on."

"Well, I don't know where you're getting on to, or where anybody's going. Two of your brothers are gone, and Wayne is still at loose ends, and your sister wants things she will never be able to manage. And now, you. God has punished me for ever marrying."

"Mama, you're too anxious about us. Wayne will find himself and Elnora is just a normal girl who would have been happier in the big city with a little more glitter. As for me, I really want to do all the big things you hoped we would. With Sted, I can do some of them. I don't think there's anything wrong with the way I feel about marriage. Somehow, I feel something is more important than what people usually talk about, something to do with the dual nature of God."

"Dual nature of God? You leave God out of this!"

"But I can't. God is Love and love is reciprocal. There has got to be two and a marriage somehow in God."

"We're not supposed to ask questions of God."

"Well, I'm going to."

"What I want to know is what was Sted doing all those years before he came to Houston?"

"Do you want to hear how successful he is as an artist?"

"I want to hear about his women."

"There was only one, as far as I'm concerned. He had a letter from her just a couple of weeks ago. He wrote back that he was going to marry me."

"Well, if your marriage doesn't work, just remember that it was just as much your fault you got married as it was his."

I became Mrs. Wilfred Stedman on November 15, 1928.

Two days after Sted and I were married, a beautiful and smartly dressed lady came to the studio. Sted was pleased and all smiles. She was a cousin of "the lady known as Lou," as he always referred to the New York girl with whom he'd been in love.

This cousin lived in Houston and was indirectly responsible for Sted's involvement with the community. She had just dropped in to say hello and see his new home, which was pictured with a write-up in that month's "Civics for Houston" magazine and featured as a bachelor's apartment. When Sted introduced me as his wife, she seemed embarrassed. I was sent to show her the upstairs living quarters.

"You look awfully young." I'm not sure she didn't ask me outright how old I was, because I remember I certainly felt like a child in her presence. She added, "I'm sure there must be something special about you, because Sted is smart."

Downstairs again, Sted met us and walked her to her car, and stayed there talking with her much too long for my nervous system because I was afraid, all too soon, that we had made a mistake. When he came back in, I was tense and unhappy. But we didn't discuss it.

In the year that he was courting me, he'd told me about the relationship between himself and the lady known as Lou. When I mentioned her once he snapped, "Why did you have to bring her up?"

A little later, when his friends came to see us, I had no cigarettes or alcohol to offer them. Sted told them he'd found me barefoot in a corn patch, which burned me up. But privately he was glad that I didn't smoke or drink, and he said that he didn't care for the stuff. Now I was being laughed at for being unsophisticated.

Sted finally found some liquor for his friends but when he went to make drinks he couldn't pull a single ice tray from the refrigerator because they were frozen up. He came storming into the living room to get me. His friends retreated to the garden.

"A fine wife you're turning out to be!" he shouted. "You haven't defrosted this thing for six weeks."

"You used to do that. Why haven't you done it?"

"That's your job now that you're my wife! And keep your voice down or they'll hear you. Do you have any lemons?"

"No, I haven't any lemons, and maybe you'd better get yourself another wife!"

I managed to get the ice tray out, but tears filled my eyes.

"You big baby. Go fix your face."

"I'm not going anywhere, and I don't care what you tell them. You can just buy cigarettes and snacks and lemons yourself."

With that, I went to the bedroom and shut the door.

The next day, he was out in the garden staring at nothing. I went out with my hat on and my purse in hand and put my arms around him.

"I'm going shopping. Would you like me to get some cigarettes and lemons?"

"Yes, would you do that for me?" he asked sweetly.

I kissed him and he hugged me tightly.

"I'm glad you kissed me. I don't want us to quarrel. And be careful driving."

We kissed again and both felt relieved. A few of his friends began to like me and I liked some of them. He said I drove the others away.

He thinned my friends to the bone, too. There were no more lonely nights for either of us, though. Before we were married he used to sing:

"Just me and my shadow, all alone and feeling blue..."

Now he sang:

"Margie, I am always thinking of you, Margie..."

and...

"Blue Skies Shining at me, nothing but blue skies Do I see..."

He sang and laughed in a tone I had never heard before. But soon, he began to sing a different tune:

"Just Molly and me, And baby makes three, we're happy in my blue heaven."

Our child, Tom, was a nine-pound boy, born on Labor Day, September 2, 1929. My mother said it was "union labor" because she, my father, and Sted were all there.

One day, the cousin of the old flame came again, to see the baby, and brought a pretty little dress for him. With her was her ten-year old daughter. Sted made a big fuss over the child. He hadn't seen her for more than two and a half years. As the lady was leaving, she turned to Sted and said:

"Well, it looks like your marriage has turned out all right."

"Well, I had to marry someone."

Yes, he used to sing to me, "Well, I had to marry someone and it might as well be you..." There was music and fun in the way he sang it, but he wasn't singing now. It was a flat, colorless statement.

"Why doesn't she stay away and leave us alone?" I said to my nurse who had just come into the room to get the baby.

The little girl ran to catch up with her mother. She had been standing beside me when I asked the nurse that question.

We never heard from the cousin of the lady named Lou again.

Sted was fond of breaking the silence in the studio with stupendous remarks, such as: "If you had to name two desires that motivate people the world over, what would they be?"

"I don't know. What would you say?"

"Preservation of life and the pursuit of happiness...and do you always have to say 'I don't know' to everything? You could answer if you would just stop and think."

I wasn't good at giving quick answers. I had a childlike faith in a world where happiness wasn't hard to find if you looked in the right places, and that search, in itself, took care of preservation.

I began to think of my mother singing as I used to hear her on a clear sweet morning. She was out feeding the chickens or sorting clothes under the ash tree. "Count your many blessings," she would sing, "name them one by one."

"All right, Mama," I said. "One, there's you and my father. Second come my own brothers and my sister. Third, the background environment which held all the things I loved as a child: the community, the church, the school, my playhouse, the big white mercantile store, the powerhouse, our friends and their homes, the prairies and the skyline, the trolley, the woods and the turtle doves. Fourth, my art studies, and fifth comes you Sted, you and me. Already we have a home of our own and a baby boy. I am happy and I will be happy as long as this goes on..."

CHAPTER 2

It was in Illinois that my father and mother were married, and where all except one of us were born. I was the fifth, next to last of six children and by then they had run out of tall stature and blue eyes. I was small and dark and scrawny and wondered whether I should cry when I looked in the mirror. But I was the only one to have my father's dark eyes, and Dad called me his black-eyed Susan.

My immediate family moved by train to Texas in 1908 when I was a baby. My father was a builder, and was attracted to Houston because he had heard that it was destined to become a big town where there would be work. He left our home in Charlestown, Illinois, to look the situation over, found a house to rent in Harrisburg and then wrote for my mother. Mother carried me in a lunch basket and the conductor was sure I was a dog she was smuggling onto the train. Her eyes dared him to touch me and he went his way.

We stayed in Harrisburg for a while, then moved to a house on Brumner Street. In one day and out the next. Bedbugs.

Our next home was in the country, a place called Bellaire, ten miles west of Houston and about a mile from where my father was building houses for the Westmoreland Farms Corporation. The house was a two-story unfinished frame structure, still smelling of new wood, with a barn and a lone tree in the back yard. Across the road from us was the Teas Nursery. Tall prairie grass reached to the horizon all around the community, except for a small span of woods in one direction.

That house and the land around it were the beginning of my childhood memories. I was just beginning to walk, and a little pig ran right between my legs and gave me a ride the first day. I remember being rocked to sleep on my mother's lap in a big rocking chair, the floor boards creaking. As she rocked she churned butter in a tall crock with a long-handled dasher, singing sad lullabies. In those days Northerners weren't very well received in the South. The Civil War was still fresh in memory. She missed her father and brothers and her half sister terribly, and her sixth child was then on the way.

The baby was born in the frame house. The doctor came from Houston on one trolley car and went back on the next, an hour later. Harrell was skinny as a rabbit, and not at all pretty until he dined for several months on Eagle Brand Canned Milk.

I loved the house and the smell of new lumber. My sister hated it. Things began to look up for my mother and sister when we moved into one of the new finished houses in the heart of Bellaire. The older houses of the community were Victorian gingerbread, with verandas running along two, sometimes three sides, with turned balustrades and lattices and a lacy fretwork facade on the pitched roofs and porches.

These houses were elegant: women's houses. But there was no elegance to our own new house save my mother's grace. Although well-built, finished with dark brown woodwork, a fireplace, bookshelves and even a couple of stained-glass windows, still it was plain, as functional and ugly as a Morris Chair. This was the era of the birth of such houses—the American bungalow.

The year 1914 arrived. Thoughts of war cast a black shadow over our homes. The following year brought an unusually violent and destructive storm, during which my brothers were wonderful: "Shut all doors, push heavy furniture against each one! Take up the rugs, lay the vases down, and anything that might shake over and fall."

Tommie rolled the piano against a door. I was hoisted up on top by Ralph, who shouted above the noise at my mother to never mind the pictures swinging on the walls but gather round the piano. He sat down and with a grin on his face began to play a song, a lullaby, to appeal to Mother Nature's better side. The storm's heart softened and flashes of lightning gave way to dawn.

We judged our good fortune by the misfortune of others. We learned that women in silk nightgowns had been driven from their homes through the blackness into drainage ditches where they and their husbands pressed children against the banks, their bodies shielding them from flying debris. The storm had leveled houses, leaving only brick fireplaces standing amid a shambles of boards. Our own house fared better than most, it was only moved on its foundation, and had settled a little drunkenly on and off its foundation blocks.

After the storm there were the houses to be repaired, and the war in bold banner newspaper headlines, plowing and tilling the ground for seeds of hatred. Would the United States get into it?

"Sure we will, and the sooner the better," said my two oldest brothers. They couldn't wait to get in their personal licks.

"You don't mean it," said my mother. "Your own great-grandfather was from Germany."

There had been a German family in the community from a long time back. Their small house, which I dearly loved, was strongly built of rough-sawn boards nailed up and down with four-inch battens over the cracks. The roof was shingled, sloping down over a part of the back where there was a lean-to kitchen all weathered to a chocolate brown and surrounded by roses and trees.

A whispered story about the house was that the German woman had helped her husband build it. She worked like a man and wore overalls, and was even seen on the roof helping him shingle it. This was a disgrace to the neighborhood women but in spite of this the people took pity on the Germans and all went one day to give them a hand. The women of Bellaire took food which we ate in the yard from a big table made of boards and sawhorses. This was before the war broke out.

Afterwards, the Germans left our community, perhaps going back to Germany. "And high time," everyone was saying, "with the war on and everything." My oldest brother Tom bought that little house for his bride-to-be.

The wedding was beautiful. There he was, standing with his arm stretched out straight, his bride standing underneath to show how tiny she was and how tall her husband.

Just one month later, I was in the yard at home when some electric-linemen and a black man drove up in a truck and asked for a rope. The old black man who had been freed from slavery by President Lincoln was the only one I recognized. He was shaking and weeping, "Ain't never loved nobody like Master Tom."

"Master Tom," my brother, an electrician, was dead. He had been working with these repair men from Houston, repairing the Bellaire trolley cable. The old black man had seen the streetcar coming and had run shouting to my brother, but the wind was strong and it was too late. The current passed through Tommie as the trolley passed beneath him. Tom's lineman's rope was needed to lower his body to the ground.

A little over a year later we had just finished breakfast when the famous flyer and flight instructor, Eddie Stinson, came in and told us there had been an accident. My brother Ralph, his student, had been hurt. Ralph had made his first solo flight that morning, and something had gone wrong with a wing before he gained height. The plane was all over the ground, shattered. We had to pass it on our way to the hospital.

Ralph had enlisted and the day before he was killed his commission to fly had come from Washington. This was the brother who had played the piano in the storm, the one who had spent years building model airplanes and drawings of motors that no one had ever seen. While the casket rested on its frame in the living room, I stood outside by the woodpile sobbing.

Then the casket was draped with the American flag, transferred to a caisson and drawn by white horses to the cemetery. It seemed every car in Bellaire and from Houston was in the funeral motorcade. A company of soldiers and people walking accompanied the procession. A full military service was read at the grave. Ralph was the first war casualty from the Houston area. That day the enlistment office was busy with young boys and men signing up for wartime service. Ralph's death spurred an already swollen charge.

By mutual agreement with Tommie's widow, we moved into the

little chocolate-brown house the Germans had built. It was small, but our family had been cut down and it brought the remaining members closer together. Here were trees and a pond where the Germans had raised frogs for the market in the city. Close by were the woods, carpeted in deep green moss. There were old hollow logs and wild violets and purple water lilies and a thicket of tall saplings.

Here I took solace.

Chapter 3

By 1916, we had a large "war garden." A fat man with a team of horses came and plowed on both sides of the house. Mother always talked to everything she planted and told it to grow, whether a rosebush or a cabbage plant. And the garden grew so profusely we had food to give away, to pack and dry. In short, all we could eat and more.

On Sunday, soldiers from nearby Camp Logan who chanced to hike out our way were invited in to have dinner, play croquet, and sing around the piano. One day Mama saw a young soldier strolling alone. She turned to me and said, "Go up and walk with him a bit, and if he's nice ask him to dinner." I ran up and walked with him a short way and we sat down on a railing on a bridge. He carved our initials on the railing with a heart around them. Then he went his way and I went home.

Mama said, "Where is the soldier? Wasn't he nice?"

"I don't know, Mama. How can you tell if a boy is nice or not?"

My sister Elnora and her friend each had a steady soldier boyfriend who visited regularly at the house and there was always a crowd around the piano. They sang war songs, patriotic songs. I hid my head under the coats piled on the bed so that I could not hear the words or I went to the woods and stayed until dark.

At school I couldn't help but hear rifle practice all morning. The children played war and the adults talked war and they all sang. Community life was all for the cause now, no time for quilting when there were Red Cross bandages to roll. There was also a shake-up in the school with a lot of squabbling, and a recently established second church was separating everyone in town. The community was split wide open. War seemed everywhere.

I hated this split and the songs and flag saluting we had to do in school. One night I knelt at my window and looked towards the woods and the moon and I prayed:

"God, save the one I am to marry. Keep him whole and bring him back from the war to me." It was my first secret fantasy. I was only eight or nine, but my husband was in the war.

Later, a new girl, tall with wiry blond hair and green eyes, moved into the house behind ours. With her were her bully brother and a set of twins. One of the twins had a metal pipe in his neck that he breathed through. She had a mad protective passion for him, and if any of us lifted a finger against him she flew at us like a wildcat. He was so spoiled we often tried to get away with a poke at him.

My feeling of aloneness and the tranquility of my playhouse was completely disrupted now. With these children I played ball, climbed trees and wrestled in the tall grass. We caught crawfish, and they took them home to boil alive in a bucket, yanking their tails off when they turned red and eating them between slices of bread and onions. They dumped some of the live crawfish out to the chickens and laughed at the battle that went on. Disgusting, but their roughhouse plainly told me that they knew something about life that I didn't, and that promised tantalizing excitement.

Another girl in the neighborhood, Ethel, was a mischievous red-head with dark brown eyes. For hours, she sat reading stacks of "True Story" magazines. There were two more girls who came. They were sisters. They knew secrets and lived in an uncompleted house with uncovered stud partitions you could see through. Their father said they should know things "within reason." I reasoned I should know, too, and watched while they wrestled together, using a banana as a prop. It triggered such a response in me that I vowed if husbands and wives were sinners to do that, then I was going to be a sinful woman and find me a sinful man.

I watched flies on the window pane and grasshoppers on the mullions and thought how it must be satisfying to be a woman grasshopper. I heard our milk cow bawling and watched my dad take her away and bring her back. I saw a bull jump a fence like a deer and mount a cow which had been bawling in a pasture. She munched grass as she was mounted, acting completely nonchalant about what was going on at her back.

My mother kept hens and a rooster. The rooster would spot a hen and go after her. The hen would run squawking and there would be a great to-do but sooner or later she would suddenly squat, lift her tail and expose a target spot where her feathers separated like the petals from the center of a sunflower. She would spread her wings for the rooster to tromp on while he hung on the skin of the back of her head with his beak. He would protrude what looked like a carpenter's auger and I guess that's where the saying came from that he "screwed" her. Then it would wind back into him and he would stand beside her ruffling his feathers and looking tall.

I could see the spot reverberate as though she was working into the center of her very being that which he had left her to deal with, and I also saw a hallucinated look in her black round eye and knew that she liked this fuss. This was all front to back but the girls with the banana were front and front and there was a great munching at a flat breast until there were two red spots. So, I learned a few things as the girls' father had figured was "within reason."

All of this was driven completely out of my mind by another thing, a violin case standing on end in our living room when we came home from town one day. Uncle Al had come for a visit! He was a violin-maker. He made the instruments from wood taken from old aqueducts. Water running over the wood for years put music into the wood, he said.

Tall and thin, he gave the illusion that he was stooping through the door. He wore glasses, dressed colorfully, and had a head of strong, straight black hair. We all loved him.

We had supper, and then he played his violin until it was very late.

He played gay things, lively, fast, funny pieces, tunes that Mama and Daddy knew from way back, that made them look at each other with a happy gaze, the first since my brothers' deaths.

Days and days followed. Sometimes, Uncle Al and I sat on the bench that circled the big ash tree in the yard, and he played classical music, the first I had ever heard. It reverberated in the leaves of the trees and I imagined animals dancing to it among its branches.

Just after we moved into a new unfinished house we were building, I contracted influenza and was kept at home out of school. I was very sick. Others were dying of the disease. Uncle Al's music came and went in my head. Strange pictures, too. I kept seeing images and saying to myself that I must remember to paint. There were dark and earthy colors, greens with strange golden lights running in and flooding them and figures of children and animals flashing in and out.

Both Mother and Dad had always encouraged my every squiggle. She bought me paints and brushes, my father built a studio above the main room of the old house for me and with my soup, I got a poetry reading from mother's favorite collection of Emerson.

I started to go back to school the day the Armistice was signed. The conductor of the trolley car, Old Dad Tedford, brought the word. All the school children were sent back home to get their parents. He waited on the tracks until we could get back, so that we could go to Houston for the celebration. The streets were full of people. Bands were playing. A huge parade appeared out of nowhere.

But, to me, this was madness. Though the war was over, all I could do was cry.

By the time I was sixteen, all the girls and boys of the community who were my age had stopped pulling hair and had paired up. One boy had pulled my hair but that was all. My sister insisted that I give a party so I halfheartedly sent out invitations. But the day of the party there was a new boy on the trolley. He looked at me. When I learned that he was a cousin of a girl I hadn't asked to my party, I immediately wrote her an invitation and added a postscript: "This includes your visiting cousin." The invitation went posthaste by my younger brother Harrell on his bicycle. This boy made my party a success.

My time had come, as my mother promised a long time ago. Now I was a part of community life with a boyfriend. It was 1926 and I was in my last year of high school.

That winter was memorable. There were enough of us the same age for dancing, roller-skating and picnics. Most of the time there were just four of us—a girlfriend, myself and our two beaux. Mine was called James.

The other couple was serious and urgent, the two of us reserved. The first time James kissed me we were in a crowded car. He began to plead that he didn't mean to do it. That made me angry, but not too much. Neither did I give him any help.

Ahead, there was a fork in the road. Everyone expected us to join hands and take the road together. But I knew I had to go alone. My road led to Missouri.

Early that year I had a prophetic dream about my brother, Wayne. He was sitting in a chair with his head in his hands. In the dream I walked into the room and he reached up and pulled me down into his arms and cried. The next day the dream came true. His wife, Gertrude, died in childbirth. My brother and his wife had been childhood sweethearts, there had never been anyone else for either of them. Once again our family was plunged into grief and confusion.

A restlessness seized us all, taking the family to a farm in Missouri to start a new life. But I was left behind for a while with my sister and her husband so I could finish school.

When I left Houston to go to the farm I said goodbye to my young man, but the sound of it grew faint up in the Ozarks. I hadn't reckoned with the probability of mail. Somehow, he could write much better than he could talk, and I hadn't anything to do but write back. Not that there weren't boys around, but they said "us'n" and "you'm" and "we'ums" and looked altogether too wild to suit me.

Wayne had nothing to do, either, except work on the farm with Dad, so we drove to neighboring towns on Saturday nights to dance. It was fun driving in Missouri over the low hills on a moonlit night with him, but it wasn't the answer for either one of us.

Then James came up from Houston, unannounced, as quietly as the Sunday morning sun. Together he and I walked the woods, inspected the farm, fed the chickens, shelled corn in the crib, washed his clothes, ironed them, danced a bit, and sat in the swing or on a log on the "west 40" in the yard of an abandoned house. He pinched my arm and looked long into my eyes when I would let him. We went down to draw a bucket of water from the open well and he told me to look into the well and make a wish. I wished I knew when he was going home.

He said, "Your father wants to give us the "west 40" and the old house that's on it."

I let the bucket down in the well gently and sat down on the wellhead and held onto the rope.

"You're so sure of what you want, I was afraid to tell you," he said. "But I have to know."

Sure of what I wanted! I felt as helpless as the bucket floating on top of the water down in the well. But I had a feeling that I was to marry a man who could push me under the water a few times, somebody who already knew a lot about life and from whom I could learn.

"You are an angel the way you are," he said.

"A fallen one, maybe. I'm not satisfied with myself. I feel I have a lot to learn."

He went back to Houston puzzled.

My dad said, "Well, we got rid of him, didn't we?"

"Didn't we? Looked to me like you were trying to keep him."

"Not if you don't want him, my Black-eyed Susan."

But I did miss the boy. How does a girl know when a boy is nice?

I thought of the cute little house and what fun it would be to fix it up. I wrote and told James I would marry him if he would come back. All week I felt half engaged and half crazy for impulsively writing and mailing that letter.

The following Saturday we went to Willow Springs for mail and supplies. At the post office, the letter was handed back into my hand. I had mailed it to myself!

Shortly I began to realize that the back-to-the-farm idea was dead. The crops of millet, wheat and tomatoes were lush, but there was no market for three-fourths of our harvest. Bankers from Willow Springs came out to the farm. We were practically broke and owed money to the bankers on a note. Wayne left to go back to Houston to find a job and send money.

Poor Daddy! He had seen a way, he thought, to bring new blood into his back-to-the-farm idea. He had been the one to suffer the most—all the wasted time, money and effort. We would all have to return to Houston where he would be assured of earning money in his trade to keep us all alive and where I could get into art training and work.

Chapter 4

While we were still in Missouri, my brother-in-law wrote me about "Sted." He wanted to introduce me to him before I left Houston because he knew I wanted to get into art training and Wilfred Stedman would be the artist to know—he was an art educator, a freelance illustrator and painter with a downtown studio with a good reputation.

My family wouldn't be able to leave the farm for a while, so I sketched this and that and imagined myself an artist. And I fell in love with Sted, about whom I knew nothing at that time. This activity and my imaginary love affair kept me busy until we left. All the fruits and vegetables and sorghum molasses that we had made and canned went to pay off obligations. We took some things, but the rest we just walked out and left as so many others had done before us in the Ozarks.

Material necessity and the reality of being back in Houston soon made me forget my love affair and I met him without thinking of anything but what he might teach me about art. He gave me some drawing problems and asked me to work on them at home, then bring them in for criticism. Each time the problems were finished I took them to him and he stopped his own art work to see my progress. One day he telephoned and asked if I would like to come in to the studio and do some work. I gladly tackled a poster he had set up for me to do. My lines were fuzzy with blobs suddenly appearing in unlikely places. He had spent half an hour telling me how to do it, then how it should have been done, while removing the blobs and cleaning up my lines. His encouragement, and the way he pulled a brush full of color straight and true across the paper thrilled me. With a steadier hand I was able to progress and was completely absorbed. The days turned into several weeks.

One day a girl came into the studio. She had been there before to talk to Mr. Stedman about art. They were discussing the work he was doing at the time when he playfully leaned over and kissed her.

She laughed and said, "I wasn't hinting for that."

I felt myself begin to burn as I remembered that I was in love with him. The Houston noon whistle blew and I hurried for the door but the girl, Callie, called to me and said she would walk over to the YWCA cafeteria with me. I tried to control my feelings, glad that she had to watch where she was going as we hurried along through the cafeteria line. She was a simple, sweet person, an artist herself, and full of chatter. During that lunch, without opening my mouth except to eat, I learned what I needed to know about Wilfred Stedman. She liked him a lot. (I kept my eyes on my plate.) She would marry him if he were only a little taller.

At the end of the day, as he was standing beside me in the studio and without looking at him I mentally calculated that if I took my three-inch heels off and he took his one-inch heels off he would be about three inches taller than I. I had a giddy feeling about the rest of his proportions, as though we were two halves of the same piece of fruit. He seemed mesmerized at that moment, as though he might have read my thoughts.

A few days later he suggested that four of us go on a sketching party and picnic for Sunday. I told him I had a date with someone (which was true), and asked, "Should I bring him along?"

"Well, no...that spoils it all, because I'm asking you to go with me."

I broke my date and went with him and the other couple, making myself as attractive as the occasion, nature, and my conscience would allow. We sketched a lake and went swimming in it and ate and laughed and talked for hours.

In the back seat, on the way home, he said, "It's getting dark. Get ready to be kissed. You wouldn't try to stop me, would you?"

"Nope."

"How about that date you had? You missed some kissing this afternoon, so I thought I'd just do a little pinch-hitting for him. Did you miss him?"

"Hadn't even thought of him."

"Well, in that case, maybe I can kiss you now."

He did, and turned me loose to give me a chance to see how I liked it. It wasn't a dry peck on the cheek and it wasn't too long and wet. It was full and moist, right on my lips. It was frank and honest and comfortable.

My mother always said, "Either you like it or you don't."

I liked it. And he said, "I've been wanting to do that ever since you came to the studio."

When we got home, the evening was early, so we went to a movie. During the show he held my hand tucked under his arm in such an inconspicuous way that no one could tell.

———

We looked forward to every Sunday, and to the evenings. Sometimes I would stay in town, go to supper and then to a show with him. When

I joined the evening art classes at the Houston Museum of Fine Arts, he always took me out and then later called for me, to take me home in his little Dodge roadster. There was always such a right feeling when I was with him. Soon, he told me I was the best friend he had, and that he'd told me more about himself than he'd told anyone.

He was born in Liverpool, England, in 1892, and immigrated to Canada at the age of eleven with his parents, five brothers, and a sister. He described the fun he'd had in Canada as a boy, the hard winters there and the paths he had to shovel through six or eight feet of snow. He told me about narrow escapes from whirlpools in the river, and about skating for miles over ice so thin that it sagged under his weight.

At the age of fourteen, he was apprenticed to an architectural firm in the province of Manitoba. It wasn't long before he was head draftsman, picked over men that had been there much longer.

"I was just a boy. I was washing my hands at the basin one day and one of the men said, 'Good Lord, look at that boy's hands.' I turned them over and around, thinking there must be something wrong with them. The man laughed and said, 'I mean the width and size of them.'"

They were wide, the fingers a good length, a good pair of hands. I remember them still, reaching to turn off the ignition of his little roadster while I sat on the porch waiting for him.

He wore brown English tweeds. His shoulders were wide and his step strong in classical brown polished shoes. He wore glasses over his wide-set eyes and bushy eye-brows above, which he said was the sign of an architect. "All the architects I've known had bushy eye-brows." He also wore a neat mustache, a nice shirt and tie.

A good pair of hands and a good body to go with them.

Sted had worked for architectural firms in Winnipeg, Canada, Chicago, Madison, Wisconsin, and Milwaukee, while finishing his schooling and attending art school which he began to prefer rather than architecture as a career. He went to New York City and attended the Art Students' League. When the United States entered the First World War, he enlisted for service as a Canadian, and was on the first boat sent to France, attached to the English army in the Eleventh Engineering Division.

Because he was an artist, he'd been given the job of camouflaging tents and equipment for his division right after landing in France. His division followed behind the heavy fighting, repairing railroads and bridges. "The amazing thing was that each time we moved into a new location the bombs fell where we had just been."

"We were just a lucky outfit."

Remembering my prayer, "God save the man I am to marry," I said simply:

"You had a good camouflage man."

Toward the end of the war he was a topographical draftsman, doing visibility and relief map work in General Pershing's office. After the armistice was signed, he stayed in France, studying anatomy at the medical university in Besancon, living at a sculptor's home, where Victor Hugo had once lived, and painting with a French group of artists in the countryside.

The medical school wasn't his idea. The United States couldn't afford to bring back all their men at once so they offered tuition free to those who would stay over there to study. Sted had signed up to go to the famous Ecole des Beaux Arts, but typical army befuddlement sent him to this medical school. He always attributed his knowledge of anatomy to his study of cadavers which he took advantage of after skipping the other classes as soon after the roll call as he could, though he could hardly stand the cadavers.

When he came back to the States he opened a studio in New York City and soon became a U.S. citizen because of his services in the army. After New York, he became director of Industrial Arts at the Broadmore Art Academy in Colorado Springs and conducted a United States Veterans' Bureau Rehabilitation School of Art. From there he went to Dallas, Texas, and on to open a studio in Houston where he was welcomed with open arms. He was the first artist of his kind in that area.

He told me these things as we sat on the porch at night. It was magic. My mother said she could hear Sted talking or singing to me. The songs were things we had never heard before. One, a little piece from an Irish opera, "I Dreamt I Dwelt in Marble Halls," was about a princess who was stolen by a band of gypsies and fell in love with one of them.

When it was time for Sted to go home, he sang:

> "Goodbye-eyee, goodbye-eyee,
> Now don't you cry-eyee.
> There is a silver lining
> In the sky-eyee.
> Too-da-loo, old thing,
> Too-da-loo, snapoo,
> Goodbye-eee..."

I didn't want to think of him climbing the long dark stairs of his studio loft alone. I wondered if I would ever be climbing them with him.

He told me how frightened he used to be, going up several flights of stairs to bed when he was a boy in Liverpool, after listening to the Irish servant girls tell each other macabre ghost stories before a fire in the basement kitchen where the children were given their supper tea. He had to carry a candle and the shadows and light would dance in crazy shapes on the walls of the stair-well.

Sted was naturally convinced of his own abilities. An air of confidence exuded from his whole being, even in his walk. His method of instruction was often cryptic: "This is the way it's done," in contrast to my other teacher Robert Brown's gentle "Don't you feel that this should go this way?" (He taught art at the Houston Museum of Fine Arts.) Feeling my way in art came naturally and easy to me, too.

One of the greatest thrills in my training came when Sted showed me the fundamentals of perspective as applied to architectural rendering. I could now take an architect's floor plan and erect the outside of the house from it.

We had quite a volume of this type of work pass through the studio, depicting the architect's finished ideas for residential homes to be used for advertising purposes. I learned more than I care to remember about the various styles of architecture that flourished in Houston and the surrounding areas but I was always interested in the mechanics of building.

Sted used to tell me about Santa Fe, New Mexico and the houses of earth construction. He said you would never know you lived in the continental United States. In the early twenties it was a town of 7,236 people, most of whom were direct descendants of Spanish conquistadors. There were also Indians from nearby pueblos. Sted went to Santa Fe at that time to paint with friends from his art student years. He said they were all building their own homes and studios of the earth or adobe, as it is called. He was intrigued with the beauty of the Old World look of the town, and with Taos, too, where he also had artist friends. Blumenschein, Phillips, Couse, Sharp—he knew them all. They had encouraged him to join them and he was tempted but he felt he had to go there with money because there was none to be made there.

I had always had the urge to go "West."

One night on the porch Sted said, "You know, I have the feeling that one of these days you and I will be getting married and we could go out West for a visit and paint, after we get a studio home built here in Houston.

My dad was to be the builder of that beautiful studio home on Buffalo Bayou Drive, five miles south of downtown Houston. It was a handsome French Normandy style with a rounded tower. Sted designed the house. I was the go-between, carrying plans and instructions from Sted to my dad and reporting back to him how work was progressing. I was undaunted but never quite ready for the things Sted gave me to do.

Sted had said, "When I get things planted around the place this fall, we'll get married."

When the time came, I didn't know whether to run away or stand still. He met me at his studio door one morning with, "We are getting married today" and took off without so much as a kiss for the license and a ring. I wondered what he would do if I were not there when he returned. Somehow I felt rooted to the spot because I knew if I ran away I would want him to chase after me and that only happens in stories. Besides, he was too sensible for that nonsense.

We were married at our minister's house, with only my family present. Sted held my hand tight as if to say it was all right, that he would always be around—till death do us part and often during the years to follow he was to address me as "my bride."

We named Tommie, our first born, after Sted's father and my brother Tom. Sted vaulted up the steps two at a time to take a look at him. He would look into his eyes and find them shiny black like mine. After supper, Sted picked him up out of his crib and danced with him in his arms and sang funny little songs. The baby had already learned to expect that and yelled for his just due. Sted was immensely pleased that his son would cry for him and not just for me.

I soon found that the baby liked his bath, too, and I let him play in it until he was completely exhausted, hungry for his meal and sleepy for bed.

Sometimes I laughed so hard at his splashing that Sted would quit his drawing to come up and see the commotion. He told me, "You look like a little girl playing with a live doll."

So much of my time was spent with the baby that Sted began to fuss about the meals and was short with me about the missing button on his shirt sleeve. He wished that for one day I would darn his socks for him. The next morning I heard him fuming in the bedroom, so I left the kitchen to see what was the matter. He had a lot of socks laid out in a row on the bed.

"First it was holes in my socks... now look here! There are a dozen socks, but no mates. Are they lost in the laundry? What have you done with them?"

"I have a mate for you. I was darning them."

I lifted one out of the basket to show him, but his eyes were blue and penetrating and he wasn't looking at the socks but deeply into me. He made me shiver as he took my hand and led me to bed, quoting, "Come into my parlor, said the spider to the fly."

"I was afraid you didn't love me anymore, now that you have the baby," he added.

"I love you now all the more."

"I need you and I have to have you now."

And I gave myself to him and he gave himself to me and in our hunger we were both devoured.

He left me and went downstairs, but I stayed for a long while to gloat. And mingled with my fierce joy was a feeling that I had done this thing a thousand years ago in a ceremony older than time in which the female was as much a deity as the male. There had been no complete synchronization between us until that day so I wanted to entrench the feeling that brought it about.

Whatever is firm in our mind is God, in that it controls us, for better or for worse, I decided this right then and there. This experience put me well on my way to what I wanted to know of God. That he is a two-fold deity was most important. "Let us make man in our image—male and female made he them." The thought from Genesis that we are made in their image was a tremendous revelation. And what Christ said about drinking the cup of wine came to mind. "As oft as ye do this, do it in remembrance of me." I will remember what I have just realized.

Shortly after we were married Sted had asked me, "Are you sorry you are a woman?" I thought that a very odd question.

I answered him by saying, "I wouldn't have you if I were not a woman.

Chapter 5

Sted's people were Catholic. He was educated by the Brothers. My people were Protestant. I had a year in Seventh Day Adventist School and we had neighbors who were Christian Scientists, others who were Spiritualists.

I had been a devout little girl and Sted had been a devout little boy.

His folks believed, "Once a Catholic, always a Catholic." My family believed their brand of faith was "the only way." And my mother never failed to click her tongue at the sight of a Christian Scientist, or at the Spiritualists if they should pass our house.

Sted said he was no longer a Catholic. The war changed him to an atheist, he said. I was certainly not an atheist but I didn't know what I was. My only experience with churches was terminated when the minister who married Sted and me was fired for not pressing his pants often enough. My dad was a deacon in the church and this is what he told me.

Sted was against all churches. He said Bible stories didn't come out of the established churches but out of the people. "The Bible, like any great book, would still be around regardless of churches. Churches stopped the flow of intelligence among people by use of intimidation, regimentation, ceremony, pomp and creed." He said, "a man should read but think for himself, and be able to write his own story. Who authorized but a few to speak of the things of God?" he wanted to know. "If there is a God, we should know it firsthand." He gave me a list of great books to read and discussed their theories with me.

For the time being, I was ready to forget about going to church. On Sundays we went on all-day trips to paint in the country, or spent the full day on the beach. This didn't mean that our life was by any means a picnic. The meals and buttons suffered occasionally.

"For Christ's sake, get someone to help you. My mother always had five or six Irish servant girls when we were little. Isn't there someone around you can get? I don't want you to be a slave to women's work. There are so many things I want you to help me with."

So, we found Josephine—a jewel. I was able to go painting with him far more than before. He loved to paint the docks and the activity of the loading and unloading of ships. We would go to the bay area and both paint sailing boats. We painted the cotton industry, and the black people at work in the fields.

Sted's architectural training gave all of his work structural authenticity. Besides the demand for architectural renderings of residential homes and public buildings, the Rein Company was printing fine books, and kept Sted busy doing illustrations for their publications. He needed my help in the studio regularly. In the two or three years I had been working with him, he had taught me a lot about the fundamentals of architectural design and the art of drafting. But in painting, I was rapidly developing my own free style.

We exhibited our work in the yearly anniversary exhibition at the Museum of Fine Arts of Houston, and in the Houston Artists' Gallery, which we helped to organize and operate. We both participated in hanging shows, in giving receptions at the gallery and in our own studio. I attended the night life-classes at the Museum, read everything I could find about art and talked it incessantly. I became avant-garde in my work.

Sted asked, "What are you trying to do, astound the world? I have no such notions. I remember one fellow who was a darn good painter, and then he began painting things and went into raptures about doing them.

Some of us asked him what those paintings were about. He rushed over and picked out a canvas from a great stack leaning against a wall, rushed to his easel, ripped off the canvas he'd been working on and plopped this other one down. Then he stood back, clasped his hand before his breast, and waited for us to fall dead."

"We said, 'Well, what is it?'

"'I call it Azoompa!'" And he made a great sweeping motion with his arm, and a swaying motion with his whole body, and said again, 'Azoompa!' Well, the guy was just plain nuts. Too bad, too, because he could really paint when he wanted to."

"What is he doing now?"

"I've never heard too much about him. I think he got to liking the bottle."

"But you do know some who've made good painting far out things?"

"No. There are three men and one woman who were in my classes who are big names now. But they're the ones who are doing pretty sane stuff, and have stayed right in New York or managed to get their paintings there on exhibition. These painters are far out in the front, but not painting far-out things. However, the museums like far-out things. They like to encourage anything that might promise a new movement. They'd rather miss than be left behind. So you do what you like. Who knows, you might turn out to be the leader of a whole new movement."

The way he said it sounded like sarcasm. Was I trying to jump over my shadow like I used to do when I was a barefoot girl on a hot dusty road in Bellaire? Maybe I was trying to get too much feeling into my work.

So I began to paint only what I could see and studied color, harmony, composition and technique. But, when one piece I exhibited in a local gallery was labeled by an art critic as a "crisp and meticulous piece of work," I was sore. Sted thought I should have been pleased. "Meticulous" was a word to associate with someone else, not with me. I just wasn't that way. Life was romantic; life was dream, thunderous and sweet, consistently inconsistent. My painting should be a reflection of my own feelings about life, not just a studied copy of anything!

I was the youngest of the organized Houston painters, and I owe much to the Museum Director J. R. Chilman, who liked my work and to Grace Spaulding John, who was a veteran painter, and to Beulah Ayres and others who pushed my work to the front in exhibitions.

But Sted remained the hub of my life. He was always there ahead of me with his feet planted firmly in reality. Every time he reached his hand out to pull me back from far out, I was only too happy to meet him halfway—a meeting that sent us both "Azoompa," back out into space.

CHAPTER 6

The Great Depression of the thirties hit with the crash of banks and things slowed down drastically in Houston. When money for illustrations and paintings tightened, there was still a demand for instruction, so we ran a Stedman School of Art. We had good years, and the bank failure didn't hurt us because we had put our money into Braeswood property and into some apartment houses. We felt safe in thinking of using the slack time to our advantage for a painting trip.

Tommie was getting pretty big now. One day I took him out to spend the day with my mother who was now living in the country. She picked Tommie up in her arms and held him against her full bosom. He was just beginning to talk and get around. When we got home, I was carrying him into the house on one arm and he leaned around to look into my face, and patted me on the chest saying "Little-bitty Mama."

Sted thought Tommie was now old enough to take a trip with us. He planned a painting expedition through his old stomping grounds. We would camp out in the mountains and valleys of Colorado and New Mexico.

"I want you to see that part of the country. We can get away from the Houston summer heat."

"Azoompa!" I shouted.

"With a camping outfit we can go where we please and stay as long as we like. I'll make a rack for wet canvasses and start getting together what we'll need. You can do the same. Only remember, don't take anything we won't absolutely need. I don't want to unload any ballast in order to get up the mountains with the car."

I remembered what he said when it came time to pack things, and didn't pack anything we could do without. Cooking our first meal, I heard Sted pawing through the cooking utensils.

"I can't find the pancake turner."

"No, I didn't bring one."

"Didn't bring one?! You had six weeks to think about what we'd need, and you didn't bring a pancake turner!"

"Well, it was too big and cumbersome. I thought we could use a big spoon."

"We need a pancake turner more than we need anything else! And the longer the handle, the better. We can get one at the next town..."

Sted did most of the cooking while I made up beds and took care of Tommie. Everything tasted wonderful. There were hardly any cars as we got farther out West. And no billboards! We always managed to get off the road to camp where there was water and a clump of trees. The only place I had ever seen clear running water was in Missouri. The bayou water around Houston is clear only when it is stagnant and the Brazos River was always muddy red with whirlpools. In the West the streams were clear and clean enough to drink, tumbling over rocks instead of muddy banks, and cold enough to hurt your teeth. Sted always had a swim, and Tommie was a duck about it too. Sted was a good swimmer, and he said it made him feel wonderful to exercise in the cold water. We put up the tent or just slept under stars. The smell of smoke from the campfire was sweet.

Such heavenly peace! No radio, no talk of the Depression, no fire sirens in the night, no horns blowing. We slept like babies. And when the inky blackness backed away from the rose glow of dawn, we often sat by the fire, our intensity flowing gently out and over a lake, through trees and into the darkest recesses of the mountains.

The thing I liked best was setting up housekeeping every time we stopped. We chose a spot with a good view and landscape. Each time was different, each time a thrill. It wasn't just a place to eat and sleep, it was our home. We were both intensely aware of this feeling. Several times we found abandoned, wind-swept houses that we just moved into. The nicest one was a little one-room adobe house with a corner fireplace and shelves. Across the front was a portal with vines on the rafters. There was a huge, sweeping field of alfalfa in front, and a panoramic view of mountains. Nearby there were trees around a pool fed by an irrigation ditch.

Tommie made himself at home. He had a toy tractor and made miniature roads and farms, drains and bridges. Little did we know how much he would remember this trip.

We travelled through the natural beauty of solid rock, through thunderous summer hailstorms and the huge expanse of meadows.

Sted said, "You'd think, by looking at these meadows, that they were worked constantly by thousands of gardeners. Reminds me of a story about an American in England who stopped a gardener to ask him, 'Say, would you mind telling me how you Englishmen keep your lawns looking so beautiful?' The old gardener said, 'Well, sir, I'll tell you, me lad, we just rolls 'em and rolls 'em for 'undreds of years, sir.'"

Sted began to sing:

> "Just Molly and me,
> And baby makes three,
> We're happy in my Blue Heaven..."

"Do you miss the house?"

"No," he said. "I've never been homesick for a house that I've left, ever. Maybe it's because we left so many places while I was a kid. I get lonesome, but not homesick. I can't be lonesome when you're around."

"When we get back, we'll both have some pretty good things to exhibit. Those two little watercolors you did yesterday are strong. You have a distinctive style of your own and should be proud of what you are doing."

"I like the ghost town you painted, and the little one with the rainbow and the mountains behind. That was difficult to do, but your colors and values are true."

"I just had to paint those two. Both are the kind of thing Carlson at the Art Students' League used to warn us to stay away from. 'Stay away from the spectacular. Never paint the spectacular,' he used to say."

"Would you do something for me?"

"Oh, sure."

"I want you to write on the back of the painting entitled 'Ghost Town,' 'to my ever-loving wife,' and never sell it."

"I would sell it for a hundred bucks."

"We'll never need a hundred bucks as much as I want you to hold onto that painting. And you promised! You've been telling me we ought to keep for ourselves a few good things that represent our best work."

Sted painted the rainbow on the spot, but the ghost town was painted in the tent on a rainy day. It was an organized composite of the impression he had of the mining areas. We both painted from sketches and from memory, organizing things to make a good composition. We were fast, direct. Sted's outdoor sketches were alive with movement and light, showing his brush strokes. He painted in clear, high-key tones as a rule, which he broke in "Ghost Town" because of the nature of his subject. Mine were dark and luminous with a lot of music.

We spent some time fishing with Marge Galloway and her husband at their fishing lodge on the headwaters of the Rio Grande. Marge had been Sted's assistant when he was Director of Industrial Arts at the Broadmore Academy at Colorado Springs. We stayed in a lodge by a stream which cascaded downhill so fast it sounded like a freight train.

At the Broadmore Art Academy in Colorado Springs we met Ward Lockwood and saw a show he was exhibiting. His were the most powerful watercolors I had ever seen. He taught at the Academy that summer and I asked to join his class. One of Sted's old teachers, Boardman Robinson, was teaching there too. He was one of Sted's favorites, so they renewed acquaintances and exchanged news of other students and teachers. My watercolors became stronger with Ward Lockwood. I was a much faster painter than he was. I was amazed at how long it took him to work up a strong painting. I learned much more just looking at his finished product than I did in his class.

I remember a shady patio, and my first encounter with lilac bushes at the school. The Broadmore Academy was later remodeled and became the Taylor Museum of the Colorado Springs Fine Arts Center.

Ward Lockwood had a house at Talpa near Ranchos de Taos. We were leaving Colorado Springs and would soon be in Taos and Ranchos de Taos. We said good-bye, packed up our Oldsmobile, and headed for New Mexico.

CHAPTER 7

We took one last look at Pike's Peak looming above Colorado Springs and entered the rolling farm and pasture lands. Large barns and mid-Victorian houses gave place to adobe—primitive shelters for animals, the corrals made of logs and sticks with loose hay piled on top of the shelters. The land became less verdant but more colorful—red, ochres, and browns. Fewer streams, more dry washes.

Sted said, "When you travel and camp, you don't want to be fooled by these dry washes and arroyos. If there's a thunderstorm in the mountains above them they can become raging torrents, with a wall of water coming down without warning, clearing everything in its path."

The mountains were mostly in the distance, except when we went over La Veta Pass and climbed hairpin turns through aspen, tall fir, and pine--then down into the valley again. The sky was exciting; the air clear and dry. We could see for miles. The sky could be clear and blue right next to black and threatening clouds. These Colorado and New Mexico skies opened up a whole new dimension for me as a painter.

It was almost dark when we neared Taos. Here we spotted the tiny adobe house a little off the main road west of Taos. It sat alone and empty at the edge of a huge field. The Taos Mountains loomed in the distance.

We pushed the door ajar and entered onto a dirt floor, packed hard and swept clean; tiny corner fireplace; a bench and corner shelves; nothing else. We gathered cottonwood sticks, made a fire, and moved in. There was a quietness in the little adobe, a quietness in the vastness of the land around us.

That evening, sitting before the fire, Sted said, "I'm glad Blumenschein is in Taos. The last I heard of him, he was in Paris visiting his wife and daughter. Apparently, all three are back. They have an old adobe home and studios near the Harwood Gallery. All three paint. When Blumenschein met his wife in Paris, she was already an accomplished artist and had won some distinguished medals. He not only is an artist but a musician and sportsman. He plays the violin and likes to fish and play tennis."

I knew Blumenschein had been teaching at the New York Art Students' League in 1915 and 1916, while Sted was studying there. Just about every well-known artist had studied at the League at one time or another. It is a big old five-story building on Fifty-seventh Street. Thousands of students have poured in and out of its doors and walked its marble halls.

Many of the early American painters were illustrators, and those who came out West came for material. Some who stayed also maintained studios in New York for quite some time, until they were established as painters. The Taos Society of Artists was formed in order to get their work back East to museums and galleries. The Indians are the big attraction, and of course the landscape. It's an ideal place to work. Taos painters are workers, turning out hundreds and thousands of pieces of work in a lifetime.

At breakfast Sted said, "I'd like to call on Ernest Blumenschein this morning. Sharp, Blumenschein and Bert Phillips started the whole Taos art colony. I sometimes wish I had joined them."

We drove through a big gate into a patio with a covered well before a long portal. Blumenschein had a big studio with living quarters for his wife and daughter Helen, stretching in both directions. His wife had just taken out a partition which divided a wide hall and a dining room. She had brought furniture and rugs from France. There was an air of grace and hospitality and much talk about art. Helen was off on horseback in the mountains. I didn't meet her until years later.

To find E. Irving Couse, we looked for a vine-covered ex-Christian Brothers' Mission, which was a part of his house and studio. His work was familiar to us because of the Santa Fe Railway calendars. There were stacks of Indian paintings everywhere, and drawings galore; Indian garb, Indian artifacts, and Couse sitting before his easel painting in a business suit with coat and tie. An Indian posed on a modeling stand. Joseph Sharp's property adjoined that of Couse. He came in and invited us into his studio. They had Taos so much to themselves that they all seemed to enjoy visitors. And they were always looking for a sale.

Walter Ufer we found in his yard. He had just finished a painting. His female Indian model and a child had just picked up a rug, some corn, and a basket, and left. Walter brought out the painting, which was quite large, and placed it against a scrubby tree. We sat on our haunches and compared the colors of the painting to the earth and scenery around us.

Bert Phillips' studio was a two-story adobe with blue trim on the main road little more than a block off the plaza. I remember glass cases with Indian artifacts lining his studio walls. Painters are great collectors. We saw paintings by Herbert "Buck" Dunton, too, but I don't remember his studio.

The next day we called on Nicolai Fechin. I was thrilled to tears with the verve and dexterity of his oil paintings. He was Russian and didn't speak much English but everything in his house spoke eloquently of his art. He was a great woodcarver and had made much of the furniture himself, lintels and turned posts, heads and figurines.

Then we went to Ranchos de Taos and Talpa. We found Ward Lockwood's house and then a place to set up camp in an orchard overlooking the valley toward the village, the famous Ranchos de Taos Church, and the mountains. We each painted several things, including the famous old church. We found a hot spring someplace nearby, listened to the goat bells, the sheep bleating and the church bells ringing.

We drove around and studied the details of the adobe houses, all earth-tone, beige with "Taos Blue" trim around the windows and doors "to keep the devils out," Sted told me. There were many walled patios hiding from the street with hollyhocks against the adobe. Pots of geraniums filled window sills. We went to the Taos Pueblo, about six miles out of Taos and saw the two complex "apartment" buildings of one, two, three, four and five stories of adobe with the Taos stream between the two groups of buildings.

There were ladders at every level of the buildings because there were no interior stairways. The plaza and grounds around and in between were bare, not a blade of grass or a shrub. The ground was packed hard and swept clean of pebbles, for moccasined feet and ceremonial dancing. A well-kept church faced the plaza and another was in ruins, with parts of two towers and long eroded walls standing. Beyond were the stabled horses belonging to people on one side of the river. The other group of dwellings across the river had a neat group of stables for their own horses.

There was a sentinel wrapped in his blanket as his outer garb (winter and summer) standing on each complex watching over the fields. Otherwise, there was hardly a soul about. The people were in the fields working, fixing fences, or inside.

I was speechless.

Sted said, "The artists had to win the Indians' confidence before they'd pose for painting but now they work together, each respecting the other's traditions and manner of living."

"What are those round mounds set on adobe platforms with flat rocks or boards in front of the small openings?" I asked.

"Those are hornos, ovens for baking. They have a small hole in the top to let the smoke out. The women build fires in them and when the ovens are hot, they clean all the ashes out and put their food in, then close up the entrances. The baking is all done by the heat retained by the adobe walls and floors. We will have to buy a loaf."

After seeing the Pueblo, we headed for Santa Fe. Sted remarked, "It's the prettiest drive you'll ever see. We'll follow the Rio Grande Gorge for a long way."

And when we got on the road, he said, "In the early '20s I used to come down from Colorado Springs in a Model T Ford and didn't dare travel this at night. Sometimes rocks as big as a washtub rolled down from the mountainside onto the road. I was always having to get out and roll some out of the way."

Suddenly,Tommie was carsick and we had to stop. He loved the river water, it was icy cold. And there was a lot of water because of the snowpack the winter before. The depth of the gorge and the height of the mountains through which it ran seemed magnified now that we were out of the car. We felt the roar of the river at the same time as we felt the silence.

Sted broke the quiet with, "This gorge wasn't cut by the river as you might think, it's an earthquake fault. At one time there was a lot of earthquake activity in this area. One of the world's greatest craters is not far from here."

"See the black porous condition of the substance of these mountains? That's the cooled lava that was spewed up in those eruptions. It is very soft, soft enough so that the cliff dwelling Indians shaped it into bricks for building rooms in front of their cliff caves and in their pueblos."

"The caves themselves were natural bubbles in the lava, some of them quite roomy. Bandelier is such a place. That National Monument is not far from here. We'll have to go. Bandelier is the name of the archeologist who discovered the cliff dwellings. The scientific community knew he was writing a book and was disappointed when it turned out to be a novel based on his imagination of what might have happened in the life lived there and how it might have become abandoned, purely fictional but very interesting. His main character was a lone woman. I keep thinking you could have been that woman."

"How so?"

"Never mind, just forget I said that."

"I guess I'll have to read the book."

"You can't ever leave anything alone, can you?"

"Sometimes you tell me I can never make up my mind."

The scenery distracted us at this point. As we drove on, the river left us and we saw Hispanic villages of adobe and tin roofs.

"This is chili land. You can have it red or green. 'Which would you prefer?' the waitress will ask you when you order a Mexican dish. And the usual question is 'Which is the hottest?' Sometimes they say green, sometimes they say red. That quality varies with the season. We might be seeing chili ristras hanging to dry from all of the viga ends of the houses as this is the right time for it."

"What is a viga?"

"Remember, I told you they are the round beams that protrude out from the wall on the low side. That custom came from the days when the Indians had no saws to cut them off at the exact width of the house. They were stone cut in the mountains where they grew and then they were dragged, small end to the ground, so that you will notice the protruding ends are not squared off but show the wear given them as they were pulled over the stones and rough ground. Letting them protrude affords a utilitarian purpose too; so natural to a primitive culture that it is truly a thing of beauty even without the chili hanging from them to dry."

"They cast interesting shadows on the adobe walls which tell you immediately where the sun is in the sky. If you are looking at a painting you can tell what time of the day the artist was working. I have seen a painting or two though where the artist worked both morning and afternoon with shadows going both ways in the same painting. I pointed this out to one of my compadres once and he said 'Well, that's the difference between a painting and a photograph.' It takes a practical eye to catch that. I am not sure if it ever occurred to him. If it suits an artist's composition to do a thing like that he will think nothing of doing it. I have even done that myself with the idea of changing it back in the studio."

"I know of one you never got around to changing and I like it."

We saw irrigated apple orchards and neat fields in long rows, then wide open spaces cut by arroyos and dotted by short evergreens and sparse plants, a wasteland carved and sculpted into illusionary castles.

It was the third of July when we arrived in Santa Fe. I was fascinated by the architecture, the narrow winding streets, the river running through the center of town, the tall poplar and spreading cottonwood trees, by the people and the nearby mountains.

There was a huge cloud about to descend on the town so we took the Old Santa Fe Trail toward Sunmount to look for a place to set up camp before the storm hit. I saw a little house at the foot of the hill that looked empty and inviting. We turned in and drove up the road a piece to a large stone and adobe house.

An elderly German man was there and told us we could rent the house and that he would bring us some wood. We just managed to get moved in as the storm cloud burst with fierce hail. The house was furnished with a big bed, a wood stove, a table and some chairs. We built a fire and I put a chicken in a pot to cook. That night I wrapped a stove lid in newspapers to warm our bed. Years later, this property was purchased by architect John Gaw Meem and is in the location of St. John's College which was originally part of the estate.

We spent a congenial and stimulating morning with German-born Gustave Baumann. We were familiar with his beautiful woodcuts and with the carved marionettes he called his "little people." He and Sted talked of printing techniques. I talked with his wife Jane. She was interested in the watercolors I had been doing and told me about a group of young watercolorists she thought I would enjoy exhibiting with — Cady Wells, Bill Lumpkins, Charles Barrows, Paul Lantz, Bill Morris, E. Boyd Van Cleave and Gina Schnaufer. (I later showed my work with this group in a gallery in Sena Plaza. Jane ran the gallery.)

Gustave was one of the few Santa Fe artists who wore a beret. George Blodgett, the sculptor, was another. George also wore a white smock and tennis shoes and drove an antique car. He and that car made a colorful combination.

We visited another couple, Gerald and Ina Sizer Cassidy at the corner of Canyon Road and Acequia Madre. Gerald and Sted shared an interest in historical topics as material for painting and illustrating. Their work had similarities in color palette and high-key tones. Ina wrote articles about artists. Their house, like that of the Baumann's, was a museum of beautifully crafted pieces of work, either collected or their own handicraft. Gerald had been the third artist to locate in Santa Fe.

We found Josef Bakos at the Santa Fe High School where he was teaching. His palette was more like mine, earth tones and an exaggerated emphasis on contrasts. He was a big sturdy man.

Will Shuster was still working on his adobe studio and home on the Camino del Monte Sol. He was a medium-sized man with bristly, unruly hair and a very straight back, quick and terribly blue eyes. While we were there, Wyatt Davis came in with some contraption for a giant effigy— Zozobra—that Shuster had dreamed up. The two of them were putting it together for the August Fiesta. It represented "Old Man Gloom" and would be burned to set off the Fiesta yearly festivities in late August or the first of September.

They showed us sketches. Its arms and head were to move up and down and sideways, its huge round eyes rolling by a series of ropes and pulleys. Jacques Cartier, a colorful dancer, would do the "Devil Dance" at its feet, teasing, and a megaphone would bellow out grunts and groans. Under the effigy's long white coat would be tons of tumbleweed. The Devil would fling a torch at its feet and it would go up in flames. The Fiesta would be on.

I also became acquainted with Randall Davey's work. I always admired him. We then took in the museum and I bought my first piece of Indian jewelry at the Spitz jewelry shop on the Plaza.

Six miles north we found the lovely valley of Tesuque (Indian for "spotted water" because the water appears and disappears in the riverbed). There were apple orchards—some planted by Archbishop Lamy's imported Alsation gardeners in the 1860s. Others were newly planted. The Little Tesuque and the Big Tesuque rivers supplied irrigation water for the orchards.

Sted said, "I'll take you to New York someday to see more paintings. There is more of these artists' works there than you will ever see here."

"I'd love to go, but only to see the paintings."

"My little country gal."

"Yeah, too low for high praise, too brown for fair praise, and too little for great praise."

"Well, your folks are country folks."

"I never think of them that way. Mama with her straight back and her love of poetry, geography and history, is quite elegant. But Daddy is so quiet and simple that he is somehow like the sticks and stones."

"You're the spittin' image of him."

"But my mother always had the stronger influence over me. She's dynamic, impulsive, reflective, active and outspoken, but always a lady. When she's with a lot of other women, she's the queen of the lot in a big way, like a Mother Superior or something. Do you know, she thought so much of Ralph Waldo Emerson that she gave two of her sons each one of his names. She brought us up on quotes from his writing and quotes from the Bible. And the songs she sang when we were children stick in my memory. I don't know what you mean by country."

"Actually, I admire her a lot."

"My Dad was a different person when we had company. I used to love to have company just to hear him talk, althought he usually talked too much or said the wrong things to suit Mama. Come to think of it, there has never been very much congenial conversation between them. I never before wondered why that is."

"He is no match for her intellect. She gets sick and tired of hearing those crazy old folktales he tells when anyone will listen. He insults my intelligence, too, when he expects me to believe them."

"You're too darn sensitive about your intelligence. He doesn't expect you to believe them, they're just entertaining."

"Doesn't expect me to believe them? He believes them himself."

"Maybe he does and maybe he doesn't. I suppose it's a country form of entertainment. They're just stories. But they have something in them—salt and flavor and medicine. I guess you have to be simple to see it. People have to make something interesting out of their own everyday lives. What we see as unbelievable is just supposed to be dry wit or allegory. My folks are proud, and I'm proud of them."

"That's the way you should feel. Although I know very well they don't like me."

"That's where you're wrong. What makes you think they don't?"

"Maybe it's just my imagination. Let's forget about it. Are you hungry?"

"I don't know."

"You aren't mad, are you?"

"Have to think about that."

He stopped the car and looked at me with those blue eyes of his, and gave a little laugh and a nudge. "Come on, get out and let's eat some lunch by this little stream."

I thought to myself, I hope he always turns my steam off with the softness in those blue eyes.

After two months of living in the open, painting and loving, we were on our way home. We both felt refreshed and like we had something worthwhile to take back with us. As we went down, out of the high altitude and back to sea level, I realized that I had felt so much better in the high altitude than I had ever felt in my life. I wanted to turn around and go back to the mountains and never leave.

"Don't get that idea in your head! We're established in Houston." This was in 1932.

CHAPTER 8

Three months before our other son Wilfred was born on January 9, 1934, Sted and my dad went back to New Mexico and bought a ranch in the Tesuque Valley.

When they came back to Houston, Sted asked, "How soon will your little papoose be ready to travel?"

"He isn't even here yet, you know."

"No, but will it take six months, two months, or how long? We have to begin to plan. Can we plan on getting out there in the spring, in time for your folks to plant a garden? In April or May?"

"In April he'll be three months old," I figured.

"Say about the middle of April? Let's ask the folks what they think."

My folks were going with us. They could look after the ranch so Sted and I could continue our painting.

First, we would have to put the ranch house in shape, and Daddy would be a lot of help there. Sted had five or six pencil sketches of the old adobe house. "Just as it is," he warned me, "and it's in pretty bad shape, so don't expect much."

But the sketches fooled me, they were so artistic. True, the screen doors were hanging on one hinge, the plaster was falling off in places, and all around the copings showed the adobe brick eaten away by the weather, but all I could see were beautiful drawings.

"The house sits in an apple orchard. There are peach trees, too, but they're pretty old and will soon die out, leaving the apple trees room to spread. They were planted, an apple and a peach, an apple and a peach, all over the ranch, because the peach trees mature and bear fruit and are ready to die out before the apple trees really get into production. You should see those wonderful big juicy Alberta peaches! The old owner was just beginning to pick when we got there. He told me that last year he sold nine hundred bushels of peaches right there on the place to truckers. He sells the apples to truckers, too. When the fruit's ripe, he gets a crew of his neighbors together to do the picking and loading. We can do the same."

He went on to explain, "There's no boxing of apples to be done because the truckers roll them unsorted into their truck beds—pretty high, too. And the only loss, they say, is on the top of the load where the apples bounce up and hop around and get bruised. If the truckers get them to market quickly, they don't even show the bruises and the rest of the load packs together and does all right."

"There are no black people out there. They're legally kept out so that the Spanish people get what work there is. I inquired about the women and it seems that won't be any trouble either, so we'll get you someone to do the dishes and washing, or look after the baby. Anything you want."

"It's right on the highway and there are mountains in the background. But you remember the little valley we went through on the highway before we got to Santa Fe from Taos?"

"Yes, of course I remember."

"Do you remember the Indian trading post on the bend of the road? Well, our ranch is on the same side of the highway, just before you come to the trading post or general store—whatever it is. Both, I think. The village proper is beyond our ranch and clustered around a little Catholic church. On the Sunday morning that we were there, we heard the church bell ring. I thought, Myrtle will like that. I thought how you liked to hear the burros bray and the goatbells tinkle. You're going to have it all now, kid. Are you happy about it?"

"It all sounds wonderful, but now I wonder..."

"Wonder what?"

"If you're doing this because I wanted to, or if it's what you want."

He answered, "I'm ready to make a brand new start. We'll have the rent on this house, and we have the Braeswood property we can eventually sell when things are right. I'll spend the winter seeing how much money I can make, sell all the paintings I can sell and do a little packing now and again. There's no need for you to worry about a thing."

We infused almost everyone with our enthusiasm. But some said, "I don't know what you want to go to that godforsaken place for."

Others said, "It's a mighty fine thing for you to take your folks, but I just don't know if it's going to work out like you think it will."

"Lots of fine people in this good old world," Sted remarked as we left Houston.

CHAPTER 9

On the second day we began to see the mountains. Mama and Daddy were in the new little Chevrolet pick-up Sted had bought for the ranch hauling, and we were in a brand-new car Sted had traded a large mural for. It was filled to the hilt, with Tommie asleep on top of things in the back with his arm around the bird cage. The baby was asleep in my lap and Sted was singing:

> "With someone like you, a pal good and true,
> I'd like to leave it all behind
> And go and find
> Someplace that's known to God alone,
> Just a spot to call our own.
> We'll find perfect peace
> Where joys never cease,
> Out there beneath the kindly skies.
> We'll build a sweet little nest
> Somewhere in the West
> And let the rest of the world go by..."

By the time we reached Santa Fe we were a little more than weary, but we would soon be at the ranch and able to stretch our legs. We bought mops and brooms and groceries. Sted warned us again that the house wasn't much, but he said there wasn't any use getting a place to stay in town because we could make out and it would just save a lot of time if he could be right there to work on the place every minute.

It was twelve o'clock noon when we drove up to the ranch house and the sun was shining down unmercifully on all its defects. I just leaned back on the car and cried. It was the sorriest looking mud hut I'd ever laid eyes on.

Sted, my father and Tommie had walked up to the Acequia Madre (mother ditch) to see if there was any water coming in, and to look the ranch over. Mama just stood and stared at the house, and then she threw down the bundle of cleaning rags she had been holding. I rarely ever saw her baffled or ready to cry, but I could see now that she had seen the artistic quality of Sted's sketches just as I had instead of the story of ruin that they should have told us.

I looked around at the ranch and it was much narrower than I had imagined, with brown neighbor kids standing on the strands of barbed-wire fencing on both sides staring at us. We could see just one tiny patch of the mountains from the roadway, with the orchard cutting off the view everywhere else. The orchard was full of dead prunings, tin cans, broken bottles, and blowing paper clear to the foothills.

Sted came back and let us into the kitchen. There wasn't a shelf or cupboard to put a thing on, the walls were cracked and dirty, the floor was filthy, the windows had no screens. There were two other rooms with apple-stained splintered pine floors, a large hall for no reason, but no closets and no fireplace in the living room. Sted's spirits were undaunted but mine were as black as a desperado's hat. I was weary with the trip and there was no place to lay the baby. He wasn't in the mood to be laid down even if there had been a place to put him.

If the place had a mountain view I think I could have faced anything. I just stood and stared. There was only a dirty wood cook-stove in the kitchen. Sted scouted around and found an old cupboard with three wide shelves that he brought in from the yard for us to clean up and put the kitchen stuff on and an old wash-stand with a shelf on the bottom which would help out until our things came by freight. He and my father brought in the springs and mattresses that we had brought with us in the truck, a big red chest and suitcases, and that's all there was. The baby cried and I cried.

That night as I lay on our springs and mattress on the floor, Sted brought in a candle stuck in a bottle, set it on the floor and sat down on the mattress beside me. He leaned over and put his arms around me and said, "Honey, don't be disappointed. We will make this place so beautiful you will never want to leave it."

"But there's no view and not a flower or a bush on the place, and so much to tear up and clean up before you can even start. Why couldn't you have bought a place that had more to start with?"

"No one wanted to sell," he said. "I told you that. It was either buy this place or give up the idea. This orchard is the best in the valley and will be a big source of income, and this house will be a good house when it's worked over. Remember my plans for it? You're just too tired to see the possibilities."

I looked up at the big heavy round beams, or vigas as they are called, with the candlelight touching them softly, and tried to see the possibilities. The possibilities were in Sted, at any rate, and he needed my help. He kissed my cheek, my neck and shoulder, patted my arm, and we finally fell asleep.

We woke up early to the smell of coffee and bacon. Mama and Daddy were up early, not knowing whether we'd be packing up to go back to Houston or starting to build the outdoor toilet that would be needed the first thing if we stayed. Sted told them it would be the toilet. First, they had to haul some water for Mama and me for the cooking, the dishes, the baby's bath, and for the scrubbing.

"You have to go easy on the water," Sted told us. "Use the baby's bath water for scrub water, and keep the rinse water from the dishes for washing. I'll see the well man in a day or two and get a well and pump out here. I can see that four grown-ups and two children are going to take a lot of water. Myrtle, figure out what kind of cupboards you want your dad to build in the kitchen and he can get those started after we get the toilet built. I found some slab lumber in the orchard and some old heavy timbers that are just what we need for the toilet. It will melt right into the surroundings and hardly be seen."

Sted went on to say, "The first big job I want to get to, after we get the toilet built, is this outside room for you folks, so that you'll have a place to yourselves. And we'll have this part to ourselves, except that you'll share the kitchen with us. Your part has been used as a donkey stable and storage barn for wood and the like. We'll have to tear out the old rotted roof and adobe bricks, down to the window heads, and build it all back again with more head room, put in a floor, closets across the far end, and build a fireplace so that you'll like it and feel comfortable on the chilly nights."

My mother looked submissive and my father looked willing. The kitchen door opened and, without our bidding, a small, grizzly, one-eyed Spanish man and four or five silent brown-faced children filed in. We said, "good morning," whereupon the old man smiled and asked how we all were. We asked how he was and where he lived. He told us he was our next door neighbor and then he told us that he'd built this house forty years ago and brought his bride here on their wedding day. His wife, he said with extra pride, was Irish, and he had taken her from the Catholic orphanage above the National Cemetery. She could read and write and speak English very well. We must come see them.

In the end, he asked if we needed any "mens or gomens." We had to guess he meant women.

From our reading during the past winter, we had a good background history of the people of this area. We knew that archaeologists had unearthed evidence of a substantial population of Indians here long before the Spanish came. We knew that when the Spanish came, before 1600, it was years before there were immigrants from anywhere else on American shores.

There were great distances between the two points of entrance into the New World. Unlike the later comers, the Spanish came not to make a new world but to expand the Crown's lands. There are still recognized Spanish land grants in New Mexico, and great isolation in the mountain villages. The people are Old World people, even though their blood is mixed with Indian blood that came from stolen Indian women.

The Spaniards from Spain were more advanced than the American Indians in building skills and technology, and were intent on Christianizing the natives. They were the ruling authority until the Indians raided their villages, took back their women and children, and literally drove the Spanish out in 1680. But the Spanish returned in 1693, and this time for good.

Meanwhile, the mountain villages remained isolated and besieged. Left to themselves, without even the priests daring to go near them, the villagers developed the Penitente Brotherhood, designed after an Italian or Spanish practice in the Catholic order. The new religion incorporated practical support of one another and met their deep spiritual and educational needs. These isolated villages are more in the northern part of the state than in this area.

There are many Spanish names in New Mexico, like Lujan, Archuleta, Apodaca, and Roybal, which are uncommon in other Hispanic locations.

But Frank Jimenez, who sat in our kitchen, had an Indian mother. And his features reflected this. He was immortalized by the painter Theodore Van Soelen in a large portrait, with Bishop Lamy's private chapel in the Tesuque Valley in the background.

Sted engaged Frank and his son at seventy five cents a day each. The going rate was fifty cents a day per man. They were to make some adobe bricks and tear down a wall that was in front of the house that had once been part of a portal (porch). The adobes from the wall could be used in rebuilding the folks' room. Frank's brother, Pat, was a good fireplace builder, he informed us, so he would be asked to come see us about the fireplace. We gave the children some magazines for their mother and held the door open for them to all file out again.

A neat little girl from another house came bringing me a fistful of yellow roses and asked, eventually, if we needed "gomens" at fifty cents a day. A woman came from the other direction bringing eggs and asked if we needed the same thing. A neighboring nurseryman came and wanted to give us flowers. A man and a boy and five wood-laden burros arrived, single file, at our door. The man asked if we needed wood. It was thirty cents a rack, "just to help you out." The entire morning was spent being neighborly.

A few days later I was struggling over some dirty task and there was a rapping at the door.

"How do you do, I'm Louise Callin," the woman said. "I met your husband last fall when he was out here to buy a piece of land, and I just dropped by to see if you and he would come by for a little while Sunday evening."

Their house was in Santa Fe. And so began one of the nicest

friendships we ever had. They were the owners of an old nursery in Tesuque we were interested in originally, but Sted was afraid to ask how much they would sell it for when he had gone to see them. This place he knew he could handle.

Mama and Daddy's place would be ready for calcimine in a few weeks. The first week was the worst because the men were tearing down the rotted top wall right in the midst of the windy season and adobe dust is the finest one can imagine. Not a window or door in any part of the house fit snugly, and in some places you would snicker at "snug" because you could throw a cat through the crack. I wasn't snickering, though. I was sneezing and having headaches and finding it impossible to keep the dust out of the butter and other foods. On potato salad we could pretend it was pepper, only the gritty taste gave it away.

My mother said, "I'd like to have the walls of our house pure white, because I've always wanted to live in an all white-washed house."

But Sted said, "Oh, no, you want color in these adobe houses. I'm going to calcimine it a nice light green."

After they moved into their quarters, it was time to put in the garden. We had to grub out a wild plum thicket that had just begun to bloom. The perfume of the blossoms was heavenly. My inclination was to go around the thicket but my folks were running this part of the show and, according to them, there wasn't nearly enough space without that area.

So we must have had about a half acre of garden when it was all in. We bought a cow and a calf, and the first cutting of orchard cover crop had to be cut for their feed before we could get back to working on the house. This had to be done with a hand scythe, left on the ground to cure, and picked up with a rented wagon and team.

I was doing a watercolor of this event when Sted yelled at me to come and help because it was starting to rain. I had to finish my watercolor from memory.

The cutting of the alfalfa gave more of a sense of freedom and openness about the place, because the alfalfa had been growing up into the lower branches of the apple trees. We had been completely hemmed in by a wall of greenery on three sides of the house. Now the place looked like a park. But I was told that there would be three cuttings a season, so I knew it wouldn't look like a park for long.

There was a big turn-around for the cars on the fourth side of the house by the garden where one could see a tiny stretch of mountains if one had time to look. I looked as I was walking with the baby. Sted never had time.

"Uh-huh, sure I see," he would say without turning his head. And if I insisted, he would say, "I'll look later. Let me get this done now."

Sometimes in the evening, we sat out there or walked out along the highway where we could see a little part of two mountain ranges. The barrancas and the mountains to the east of us caught the last rays of the sun and turned blood-red, hence they were called the Sangre de Cristo (Blood of

Christ) Mountains.

Sted and my Dad had just started to tear out the adobe wall between the hall and the living room to make the living room larger when our first surprise visitors from Houston dropped in. We gave them a dinner of corn on the cob and fried chicken. They went back to Houston and told friends that Sted was as thin as a rail and working himself to death, which was true. There was no stopping him.

They got the old pine apple-stained floor torn out and put a flagstone floor in the living room, built a fireplace themselves because the one the Spanish "expert" built smoked. We patched up the adobe walls, calcimined them white, put up a few pictures, and moved back in.

It was truly beautiful. The large bedroom at one end of the living room had a little native fireplace in one corner which could be seen from the living room, and there was a view of the orchard to the south, and a view through the kitchen onto the patio to the north. The kitchen cabinets that I had my father build were of native pine and looked just right. Sted and my dad built a Taos bed that could be used as a couch in the daytime and a bed for Tommie at night until we could build another bedroom. With candles and kerosene lamps the house was cozy.

Before the summer was over, Sted and my Dad, Frank and his son built another room and a double garage, extending the length of my parents' building, and joined the two sections of the house together with an open passageway. This, too, was very pleasing, sheltering the patio from hot summer winds but leaving plenty of air circulation onto the patio. Our part of the house was the south side of the patio with the orchard to the north and west, and the folks' part to the north and east.

The fruit crop came in, and a farmer arrived with some pigs he wanted to trade for apples. So a small pen was built and we fed the pigs apples to make the meat sweet, and we pulled the pen around so that they could eat alfalfa. But they got tired of eating alfalfa and apples and began pulling the chickens' heads off every time a chicken was dumb enough to stick its head through the wire of the pen.

Another farmer came for some apples and traded us a goat but the goat ate the bark off the trees and had to be tied up, and the men had to be called away from their work several times to save the goat from strangulation when it got itself tangled up.

"There'll be frost on the pumpkins most any night now," my mother predicted one morning.

The days were growing shorter. The fruit was picked and sold somehow. I hardly knew how anything was done because I was so occupied with baby Wilfred and everything else I did was so piecemeal. When the frost came and touched growing things with its magic stick, the hubbard squash was stored away along with apples, carrots, cabbages, and dried things, enough to rot and still leave us with plenty for years to come.

My mother got a special thrill from everything that was laid by for the winter. We had an adobe room lined with sagging shelves, stacks of boxes of wrapped apples, sacks of dried things, boxes and baskets of food stored in sand, and dried things hanging from the ceiling. She was ruling the roost by her natural and supernatural power. Once, in the kitchen I heard her say, "Now you just get out of here. I won't have you coming in here and giving me trouble."

I called to her, "Who are you talking to, Mama?"

"To this string of ants."

"I'll get the flit gun."

"No, you won't! It says in the Bible that man shall have dominion over all lesser things. I told them to go away."

In a very short time they disappeared. I had argued that it would just be chance if they went away, and about God and no God, and she complained about Sted's influence on my thinking.

She scoffed at the argument that Sted had made that there wasn't such a thing as a soul in the body because the surgeons had never found any. I took the baby and hid myself in the alfalfa to get away from her. There was confusion and disappointment in my heart. That night I told Sted that I wanted the folks to go back to Houston.

He hugged me and kissed me, but told me to do the best I could, because they came out with us to stay if they wanted to. As fall wore on I felt that the whole thing was that Mama didn't want to be with us. She was too independent, too full of energy and ambition and ideas of how things should be done, too impulsive and emotional to be happy with her independence stifled at every turn. She was born to be a leader and was always the leader, who shaped the habits and behavior of her family.

Her influence touched everyone. Everyone respected her.

———

Thanksgiving came, and with all we had in our larder we all had a lot to be thankful for.

But Sted never liked Christmas. He had very meager Christmases when he was a boy. He always told me, "I'll give you things when you need them. I don't want to be reminded to give presents for birthdays or for Christmas.

"And look," he said. "I've been putting out just about every cent we have on this place for you and your folks. I don't want you to spend money on a gift for me, and I don't want to buy gifts for your folks. We'll have a tree for the kids and get them a few things. I want that to be it, and I want you to make that understood to your folks."

In my home, Christmas had been the biggest time of the year for getting all the things we needed for the year. We may have needed socks in the fall, but we didn't get them until Christmas.

After Christmas, Sted said to my parents, "Now that winter is coming on, I want you folks to take it easy and rest up. There won't be much to do all winter and you've worked so hard all spring and summer and all through the fall that I want you to feel like your time is your own to do whatever you like."

My father was feeling fine, as though his work had been appreciated. He loosened up with one of his old entertaining stories. It was the one about the hoop snake that took its tail in its mouth and rolled down the hill behind the flying heels of my grandmother. I loved that story.

But not Sted. His intelligence had been insulted again. He asked my dad, "Is that a true lie or just a damn lie?"

That was the straw that broke the camel's back. My mother could contain herself no longer. The pressure of small grievances had been quietly hiding and adding up in her mind and this last one exploded the whole works and brought them to light. It all began with green calcimine and was so devastating to me that I told Mama, "You have to go back to Houston."

I greatly admired our Spanish neighbors, where every house contained two, three, or even four generations. I didn't have the slightest idea of how they managed it. I had never heard them argue, though one man did pull all of his wife's father's furniture out in their yard and set fire to it. And another time the same man beat up his own car with a sledge hammer. But aside from those two incidents they seemed quiet and genteel.

My dad disappeared without even listening to our arguments. He came back later and looked in my door at me on the bed with a compassionate look. Neither of us said anything.

Later Sted told me, "If your folks go back, we'll have to go back, too, because I'm not a farmer and don't want to be one. If they aren't here, I won't be able to paint next year for looking after the place. The chickens, the cow, the goat and everything have cost me money. We might as well all be back in the city."

He told us all, "It just looks like we made a big mistake ever to come out here." And he told my folks not to feel badly about it, and that they might as well go back now and we would go when we could sell the place. In the meantime, he would do a few things to pretty up the place so it would sell easier.

Sted gave the folks the truck and some money and they left.

I went to bed for a week. Then the boys got the whooping cough and we nearly lost the little one.

Letters and comments began to come back from my family, old friends, and church people, showing a mouth to mouth completely blown up and exaggerated story about our actions in regard to the folks.

I had never been directly involved with this sort of thing before and was emotionally exhausted. If it hadn't been for Sted and the boys, our new home, and George and Opal Fitzpatrick whom we could count on seeing every Sunday, I would have died. George was the editor of The New Mexico Magazine.

"Damn the green calcimine," I said one day.

"Don't let it get you down, kid," Sted said. For my part,I can forget your folks exist from here on out. But it's not right for you to feel bitter against them. Blood is thicker than water. They blame me and I don't give a damn because my intentions were good. So let me take the blame."

"I'm going to write them a letter which will make it very plain that it was I who sent them back and that I'm going to stick with you. And we're going to make a go of this place alone."

Sted assured me he would rather stay if I would be happy. "We could alter our plans somewhat and work it out together. With all the moving around I've done, I've never gone back to the same place."

"I know. I've been thinking about that."

"And I've always accomplished, at least in some manner, what I set out to do."

I told him, "We won't let this be an exception. We'll make something of this place."

"We might never want to leave it after we get it going well. It isn't as though we were way out in the middle of nowhere," Sted continued with increasing enthusiasm. "We'll soon have the place organized, and then we'll have time to have a show at the Museum—and to make more friends."

Working together, Sted and I felt a closer appreciation for each other. Even the boys were in on everything, including the joys and the responsibilities. But there was a gap and uncertainty where the folks had been. New friends and people would widen our horizons, be a stimulus to our plans and work.

But the more I sought out new friendships, the more elusive they became. We were Texans, newcomers in a place that zealously guarded itself against outsiders—especially newcomers from Texas.

Sted told me, "When people know what we came here for and what we can do, you'll have more friends than you know what to do with."

We had a joint show of our work at the museum, and we were asked to show in Denver, Philadelphia and other places. I was invited to exhibit with the young group of avant-garde painters that Mrs. Baumann had told me about, and who called themselves the Rio Grande Valley Painters. Art in Santa Fe or from Santa Fe was like art in Paris or from Paris.

But other things often took precedence. Sted said, "You'll have to help me, I can't do everything." So we worked together by day and sat by the fire at night. I read wonderful books to him, catching up on all the good ones. The first were Willa Cather's "Death Comes to the Archbishop" and Oliver LaFarge's "Laughing Boy."

Our plans were to look after the orchard and the irrigation and work in the studio. During the winter, we made a rug of the goat, sold the cow and calf, killed the pigs and ate the chickens, and cut down the "For Sale" sign we had put up in the heat of confusion.

I could look after the irrigation. There was no heavy work involved, just open the ditch gates and keep an eye on the water, move it around till the nine-acre orchard was soaked. We had certain days of the week to get water and so many hours according to our acreage. When there was plenty of water in the spring, the mayordomo, who watched the ditch, gave us extra time so that we could give the place "a good suck."

I wore the boots and took over this job and thought of the German woman in Bellaire who had worn boots and milked the cow and helped her husband build their house. This hadn't made the women of that community very friendly toward her. A few times I spent a whole night up in the orchard irrigating, catching a snatch of sleep now and again in the crotch of a tree while Sted slept so that he could do his part at his desk the next day.

He did a beautiful book on adobe architecture, with plans and renditions showing how the native adobe houses looked outside and inside. His illustrations showed patios, plants, and winding roads and old men driving wood-laden burros. The drawings of the insides showed rooms furnished with hand-carved furniture like the local craftsmen make. The book made a beautiful publication and put Sted's name on the impressive list of Santa Fe authors.

Soon Sted was made art editor of The New Mexico Magazine and was becoming well-known for his illustrations. He wanted to build a new house for us down by the highway in the orchard where people could find us easier. We would rent the old house after we built the new one.

Night after night that winter, I sat on the floor in front of the fireplace studying architectural magazines to get ideas for the house while Sted lay on the Taos bed telling his own made-up bedtime stories to the boys. As they got older, the nightly stories became longer. They were sometimes about a character called Old Slue-foot the Bear and, while full of fun, they always had a moral tucked neatly in somewhere without the boys suspecting it.

Tom lay on his father's arm and picked his fingers when he got excited. Wilfred lay still for two seconds, then sat on Sted's stomach, straddled his leg, or stood on his head and feet in a jackknife position. He was never still and could never listen without interrupting the story to ask questions, and he watched like a detective for flaws in it. "Little Pillfred" we called him sometimes, because he was a pill. But not too hard to take. In fact, he was just what we needed.

After the boys were tucked into bed, Sted and I sat on the floor in front of the fire and looked at the magazines. I moved over crabwise to him and we would talk about the house he wanted to build. It was late fall. The snow would soon be falling softly outside. This would be our second winter.

CHAPTER 10

"This will be the nicest house you've ever had."

He had the plan all worked out to scale and in complete detail, a mountain of work. It was all a woman could want, except there wasn't any of my blood in it. A strong wind might as well have come up and taken all my plans, sheet by sheet, off to the mountains. It never occurred to me to accuse him of being impertinent.

I didn't say anything. This feeling was new and strange to me, and only touched me lightly at the time. If he hadn't told me to think about how I'd want it, I wouldn't have had that feeling. But he had drawn me into a partnership feeling and then cut me off, just by his own confidence in what he was doing.

His plans looked good on paper. But the mountain view would be blocked by a blank wall and the living room would have a view of the highway instead of the orchard. Neither point was worth considering when I thought of the thing as a whole. I was lucky to have a husband who was so knowledgeable and who had the courage to tackle such a big project, especially with as little money as we had at the time. When we were working on the old house our money had gone as though we'd thrown it down a rat hole, yet we'd gotten some money from a Houston investment we thought had been lost because of the Depression.

Sted got the new house started in mid-summer. He saw the foundations and basement in, which he wanted adequate to sustain the heavy adobe walls. Then he was offered work with an architectural firm and he hired a man to be foreman on the building of the house. He was a nice old man but no good as a foreman. Another was tried but he couldn't read the plans without my help.

Sted said, "Why, you could do better than either, or both of them together. It's so simple a child could do it. Everything is worked out in detail. All anyone has to do is read and follow the plan."

"Me?" I asked.

"Why not? You've been reading the plans and catching all the problems. I'll go over the job each evening and discuss the next day's work with you. I can't be at work in town and out here at the same time, and we haven't the wherewithal to turn the plans over to a contractor. All you have to do is be on the job and see that the crew keeps busy and everything fits."

I knew this would not be child's play, but I was glad to put something of myself into the house. So I found a wonderful girl, Mary Martinez, to look after the boys and the house, put on my jeans, and carried the plans, a scale, and a tape line. I gave the adobe brick layers the location of doors and window openings when they were ready for them, their distance from where the finished floor was to be, and the height of their openings, all in time.

We were determined to get the right men to make the adobes. The Hispanic people were very good about this once they knew your intent.

Two good men, an older one and a helper, came from a nearby village to make the adobes. They set up a tent so they could stay while doing the work. At night, we could see them by firelight. The younger one played a guitar while the older one sang the songs he was often called upon to do at weddings or funerals. These were haunting and enchantingly beautiful.

They plowed up the old garden spot and made smooth a large area for laying out the bricks on the ground to be cured by the sun. The plowed ground was eventually shaped into mounds, then made like volcanic craters into which water was poured one crater at a time each evening.

The next morning, straw was chopped into small bits and sprinkled into the mud in the crater. The men barefoot tromped the straw until the mud and straw were mixed. This was then taken by wheelbarrow loads and poured into wooden forms which were lifted individually, leaving four bricks at a time to dry. The bricks in a couple of days were cleaned and racked so that the wind could pass between them to further dry them, then stacked and covered with boards, topped with tin sheets and rocks to keep them in place. They could make between 350 and 500 adobes a day.

I measured timber for lintels and had them cut and marked for their positions, got one of the men to adz some of the four-by-twelves for beams and to adz all of the lintels and other men to hand-plane beams and all "rough off the saw" ceiling material on one side only and to stack these out of the weather until we were ready for them.

I also located stud partitions for closets, determined the location for bathroom fixtures in the two bathrooms and in the kitchen, directed the man who was doing the wiring, the gas men for pipes and radiators, and determined the canales' locations to carry the roof water off; the pitch of the ceiling here, no pitch there; ordered more nails, more one-by-sixes, more this and that.

Fire a man, hire a man—all just child's play! The men all liked me and would do what I said, and in many cases I had to rely on their advice and give them leeway on the things that they knew better than I. They were expert masons and did their work with care and pride.

The fruit crop came in, so I took part of the crew from the house and got all the fruit down over the seven acres of trees and put a boy in charge of handling small sales. I stopped whenever a trucker came in and talked to him until he said he would take a load, and all of the crew were called to load him up and he went his way—after pinching and biting apples and haggling about the price. We sold twelve hundred bushels of fruit that year.

I was confident that I had handled two man-sized jobs, but when the house was nearly completed Sted told me that I was getting too big for my britches—in front of the men. He said he had been crazy to tackle a job like that with me handling it. I'd let them get away with murder and had caused him enough grief to kill a weaker man. He poured it on, saying he was a nervous wreck, working all day to make money and coming home at night to find things all wrong, then working on the job himself until dark.

After that I got no cooperation from anyone. Their own work as well as mine had been criticized by those words, and you just don't do that to proud people. Somehow we managed to get the job finished. But I felt tired and defeated as we shut up the old ranch house after moving the last bit into the big new one, and I recalled that my mother used to say: "Lonely women live in big houses."

I wasn't just lonely, but in a dark despair. Sted and everyone else had been amazed. People had been seriously asking me ("Not Sted," they had said) if I would build a house for them. But his emotional outburst at the end had swept everything out of my mind. I felt like taking an axe and tearing into the place, beating up and knocking down everything that I had worked so hard to see put up right. There wouldn't be anything untouched and standing on Sted's "adequate foundations" but a few segments of wall and his fireplaces, seven in all. I might knock down some of them, too, because I had held a candle for Sted while he worked on them after dark.

I was angry. I felt no better than a fishwife. I had done a good job; why couldn't I console myself? My whole body shook.

He could change from one mood to another like turning off one faucet and turning on another. I didn't know how he could do that, but the soft look in his eyes afterwards warmed me to the marrow of my bones, and I forgot about myself and thought only of him.

What he said had a lot of truth in it. It wasn't so much what he said but how he said it. I felt completely discredited. Why did he do it? When I asked myself, I got the answer: because I had been assuming too much credit. He was reminding me that I couldn't have done any of this except for him.

My childhood had been sheltered. There had been no display of emotions, no trial-and-error analysis at home. I had no intestinal fortitude for the things that were coming up in my life with Sted. I had to find some basic understanding of what I was as a woman and what he was as a man, which I expected would explain the whole universal order. It never occurred to me to say to Sted, "What's the matter with you, man?"

The new house with all its modern conveniences created a whole new world. No more washtub baths before the old kitchen wood stove by the light of a candle. I felt a little cleaner when I came out of the big white tub, but I couldn't say that I felt any warmer or more romantic. It had been kind of nice up in the old ranch house.

We would be modernizing it next spring, but I would never forget our two and a half years in that house, how cozy those long winter days and evenings with just Sted and me and the two boys, the fire crackling in the wood stove and fireplace, the teakettle always humming and ready to give forth if it hadn't boiled dry or the fire hadn't gone out.

Now that we were looking back on it, we could remember how nice it was and could even laugh at how awful it had looked the first day we arrived.

We spent the winter in the new house. Like the "gringos" we were, we hadn't had the patience to let our bricks cure for a year as the Indians and Hispanic people do, but used them as soon as they could be handled without falling apart. As a consequence, all winter long we couldn't see through our windows for the moisture collected on them. Cracks developed around each viga and beam from the drying of the adobes and from the shrinkage of the green lumber. These had to be muddied up and repainted a year later.

All winter we spent our time over and above our art work carving the furniture. We never burned a piece of lumber that was six inches or longer. Sted would pick a piece out of the fire if it got in the fire box and use it. In a few days, six months, or five years hence, it would appear in some piece of furniture or a cupboard as a carved spindle or maybe just a cleat holding up a shelf, and I'd laugh when I recognized some of the pieces. How could Sted ever feel that I didn't appreciate him? He was more wonderful than he suspected.

The native people had a tin craft. Tin out here in the thin dry air didn't rust, and they had a way of waxing it with warm candle wax that helped preserve it from stain and left it with a dull sheen. They used tin for candle holders, wall sconces, electric lighting fixtures, lamps, mirror frames, matchboxes, ashtrays, and elaborate chandeliers. The sheets of tin were cut with tin snips, stamped with dies and punches, shaped and soldered together.

Sometimes they were given added touches of color. Used with the pine furnishings and Indian rugs or blankets, they were very beautiful. They weren't expensive unless one didn't have much money (and then anything is expensive.) We wanted tin fixtures, so I learned to make them and was happy because I was using my art in a creative way. Paintings still weren't selling. The whole country remained in the Depression. If a local artist sold a painting it was front page news.

So artists were turning to practical things. Some were waiting quietly for better days, or spending a lot of time to bring about a government Works Progress Administration and then to get into it. Sted helped promote WPA projects such as the building of schools, administration buildings, and hospitals while working with Kruger and Clark and Associated Architects, making architectural renderings that showed how the buildings would look so that the projects could get government approval.

There was a lot of resentment about the WPA projects, and Sted too was worried about repercussions that might (and did) follow across the country, spending money to create jobs. But there was also a lot of good accomplished.

With electricity in the new house we had a radio again, and felt more concerned with what was going on in the world. Often in the night, in our new upstairs bedroom, I awoke and wondered who I was and where I was, staring at the dull light spots that were windows, completely lost. After the room came slowly to my mind, I began to feel the bigness of the house below me, and I wondered why we had such a big house and why we were in the West. How had it happened that I was so cut off from my family? It seemed there had been a break in my life, with no bridge connecting the past and the present or leading to the future. To find myself meant reconstructing the bridge or making up my mind to ford the new strange stream. But a stream is just a stream, and there's nothing strange about it if you know where you're going. I didn't know where I was going, or why, and it seemed to me that the whole country was doggedly following a trail that would be mixed up for a long time. My ear wasn't to the ground in that upstairs bedroom, and the bedsprings seemed to pick feelings of unrest out of the air and transmit them to my inner ear.

These were winter impressions. But winter was passing and a feeling of spring was noticeable in the air.

CHAPTER 11

We referred to the old house as the Old Ranch House, and to the new house as the Big House. In fixing up the Old Ranch House in the spring of 1937, we used all our ingenuity. Sted was thinking of the rental money it would bring in. I was secretly thinking that this was my chance to get interesting people around us.

Sted couldn't help but do things to the old house to make it attractive; I wanted to do my part. The house must be just as attractive as it could be to bring in the money for Sted, to make George Washington crack a smile and wink for me from the face of those dollars.

Sted said, "We don't have much money to put into the Old Ranch

House, so you'd better scout around in the second-hand stores and see what you can get that we could use. Look for well-made old solid wood dressers. Do you know what I mean?"

"Yes, I do."

"Then why didn't you say so?"

"I was just thinking...you want me to go in like I wasn't looking for anything special, and wiggle a chest of drawers here and a chest of drawers there—like you do to my tin fixtures to see if the joints are going to hold—and reserve my opinion of the thing as an objet d'art until the second-hand man says I can have it for six dollars?"

"That's just what I mean, only get it for four if you can. If you go in and start to raving about an old dresser, he'll think he has a museum piece and jack up the price. And I don't want you to bring in some 'sweet little old piece' that's falling apart. I don't mind doing a little repairing on something that'll be solid and useful when I get through with it."

"I'll see what I can do."

We were in good spirits because we both liked what we were getting into. This kind of work was play for both of us. He told me, "Don't look for any beds, because I think I'll have the mill man make some sturdy wooden frames. We can buy new springs and mattresses. Guess we better buy the springs and mattresses first and have the frames built to fit. He can make us a couple of armchairs and a long couch for the living room. I'll put a little carving on them and they'll look swell. You left the nice old cherry-wood table up there, and the antique chest of drawers with the mirror that goes with it. And what else did you leave in the house?"

"There's the little iron chest for blankets, some straight chairs—those fiddle-back things. What about the old cupboard with the doors on it that you found in the yard when we came?"

"That could be painted and used."

"Could I paint some colorful designs on it like you find on the old colonial furniture?"

"No reason why you can't. It ought to look pretty good if you do. All those things will look good in that house because it's Spanish Colonial in style. And someday I want to put a pitched metal roof on it and some brick on the otherwise exposed coping and make it even more Spanish Colonial!"

Sted had put a portal across the front during the second spring we were in it. I had planted hollyhocks and cosmos. They should come up again; the hollyhocks get prettier every year and the cosmos reseed themselves.

When we got through with the alterations, we had a house that was quietly beautiful and homey. Sted thought we could only get a modest rent for it because it was out of town. But I thought we could get a good rent for the same reason, and because it would appeal to people who wanted a nice quiet spot to tuck themselves away for a rest from business, since this was a resort area.

He said, "It might be all right for the summertime, but most of the time we'll be renting to working people. Sooner or later I'm going to make two apartments out of the house like I wanted to in the first place, and we'll be getting two small rentals but will keep it rented the year round."

"People who want to live in the country wouldn't want to share the house with anyone else. They want a little space around them."

"Well, we'll see how it turns out, you always seem to be opposing my ideas. But let's get it rented!"

My friend Louise Callin came out from town to see it, and she said, "It's precious, and I know just the rental agent you should get in touch with. She'll be thrilled to have such a charming place on her list. She's constantly in touch with just the sort of people who would love it."

Our first tenant was Irene Peck, a librarian, and her son Jim, and her black maid and the maid's little girl. The divided house was perfect for them and they were perfect for us. Jim was two years older than Tom but was company for both boys. Irene was a great reader and she liked to walk with us in the hills. We all loved her. Toward the end of her year's lease she found a house that was being built right out of Sted's book on adobe architecture. She had Sted make some revisions in its plan that made it right for her and bought it. She had beautiful things and kept the house open and inviting to us.

In 1938, we worked over another old house on the ranch that had a history dating back two hundred years. It was adobe, with walls two feet thick, heavy beams, and a split cedar ceiling. We used it for a cow barn the first year, and then as a place to store lumber. The ceiling was so old and tired it was unsafe.

We started to re-roof it and wound up building it into a house. Sted asked me to supervise the re-roofing. When I went up to do this I happened to have an envelope in my pocket, so while the men worked I made a sketch for turning the structure into a little studio house. When I went down to the Big House for lunch I showed it to Sted.

He said, "Do you want to do it?"

"Yes."

"There isn't room enough to build a fireplace like that, with the bancos (adobe seats) like you have them sketched—but that's a good idea to break the big room up into two areas. It gives a living room area, and this smaller area can be a dining area, and yet it will be just one big spacious room. Let's go up this evening and take a look at it. I don't see any problem with the kitchen and bath the way you have them planned to take off through a hall. We could add a small bedroom onto it and have a complete little house."

We went up after supper and I had him draw in the dusty dirt floor the partially projected dividing wall which would be made by a corner fireplace. Then I sat down in the dirt so he could draw around me for the location and shape of the bancos on either side. We had more than enough room to make the fireplace and the seats as I had sketched them on the envelope.

While we were working on the studio house, our Spanish-American neighbors came and sat on their haunches watching every move our workmen made because we had to dig out rotted structure to replace it with new, and dig new foundations for the room that we were to add on. The original room was described in the abstract and title as "a room with seven vigas." These watchers expected to see a pot of gold unearthed.

They told us that structure had been one wing of a big house that used to tie up with a room that was several feet on the other side of our fence, on the neighbors' property. They said that a rich cattleman had lived there, sold his cattle, and then died. No one knew where he had hid the money that he got for his cattle. We found arrowheads, stone axe heads, and many pieces of pottery. There were two pots buried in the structure but they weren't full of gold. One had a rat's nest, the other had a little straw in the bottom of it, but that was all. Hiding money in pots was the old method of banking where there were no banks.

There were ancient apple trees at the north end of the house. I had designed a big studio window and an entrance door at that end, so that when the door stood open the whole end of the living room was open to a small patio and the big trees. In the winter it was a beautiful picture, with the snow on a terrace where the trees grew. One day George Fitzpatrick came up to the house while I was helping Sted put the oak floor down in the bedroom.

"Gee, Sted, you sure designed a sweet little house out of the old cow barn."

"Yeah. You like it?"

Then and there I decided that someday I was going to design a house and get the credit for it.

Our first tenants in the studio were John Gould Fletcher, the poet who had won the Pulitzer Prize that year, and his wife, who was a writer of children's books. In the wintertime they put a pan of feed in the trees and had snow birds and blue jays there all day. The birds were their friends, and to hear them talk about them you would think they talked the same language. Haniel Long, the long-time and well-known Santa Fe poet, and his wife used to love to come out to watch the birds with them.

By the little studio house there was an apricot tree reputed to be as old as the house. It was just a haggled old stump with one live limb and a half-a-dozen apricots. I knew it well because when we lived in the Old Ranch House I used to stand at my kitchen window and look at the old thing and derive strength from the knowledge that it had withstood two hundred winters right there. There was something beautiful about it and courageous, but Sted wanted it out because he was afraid that someone would back into it some night and ruin the back of their beautiful car and hold us responsible for the damage. The tree stood at an edge of the only clear spot on the whole place large enough to turn a car around in. Yes, the tree was in the way.

John, big but slightly stooped, came out wringing his hands when the men started cutting the tree out. He pleaded for its life but he couldn't get around Sted's practical point. Sted could put a thing like that in a picture, but in the turnaround it was another story.

No. On second thought, I don't think he would even want it in a painting, not without taking artistic license to move it back six feet. On the ranch, he wanted all the trees well pruned and cared for. If a limb failed to come forth with leaves in the spring, you would soon see it lying on the ground, and a fresh saw cut would show where it had been up in the tree, no matter if the tree was a shade tree or a fruit tree.

"I didn't say anything about the tree," I said.

"No. But I could see by your eyes that you didn't like to see it go. Would you or John want to pay for a smashed-up car? You're too aesthetic."

At that time Santa Fe and Taos flourished with big-name writers and artists, and sooner or later they would either show up on our ranch or we would exhibit as one with them. John Gould Fletcher lived in our little studio; Josiah Titzell was the second to live in our Old Ranch House. He was a former editor of Publisher's Weekly for Brewer, Warren nd Putnam, Doubleday Doran and the Conde Nast Publications in New York City. Lynn Riggs the playwright, whose "Green Grow the Lilacs" formed the basis for the musical "Oklahoma," took a little house next door. We were invited to sit in on poetry readings, or they would find their way down to our studio. I made portrait sketches during these sessions while the others talked books and art.

Up the valley from us was the Rydal Press. Walter Goodwin moved its operations from Pennsylvania to Santa Fe in 1933, the year before we came, with the express purpose of publishing regional literature. Each author paid for the publication of his or her own book; it was the first self-publishing authors' press in the entire country. Goodwin was invited to come here by a group of writers which included Haniel Long, Peggy Pond Church, Alice Corbin Henderson and Witter Bynner. They "sought freedom from the dictates of the Eastern publishing cliques that determine what shall or shall not be published." (This quote appears in an Ancient City Press book, "Santa Fe and Taos: The Writer's Era 1916-1941.")

I was happy with our community. We had people on our place that we could eat Thanksgiving dinner with. They were our guests for Christmas dinner, too; beer and songs in the summer evenings, and outdoor suppers. There were often children who were company for the boys, and we were all together doing rope tricks, pitching horseshoes, or lying on the grass around a fire, telling stories in the moonlight.

Sometimes we tramped around in the hills in back of our place to watch the sun go down over the Jemez Mountains and then watch the moon come up over the Sangre de Cristos. In the bedroom at night Sted would ask me if I was happy. I could utter no word. I just hugged him close.

In 1941, famed Southwestern writer Oliver LaFarge was living in the Old Ranch House with his wife Consuelo and writing on a grant. One night that year he threw pebbles at our bedroom window screen.

"El Nido is playing Spanish music," he said.

We went down in our robes to find the Wyatt Davises with them, then went out to the highway arm in arm, and danced the varsoviana in our bathrobes on the highway between our house and El Nido. I with Oliver and Sted with Consuelo; my robe was a full red thing that flared to the dance.

El Nido was about three hundred feet down the road from our house. It was the place to go in those days for drinks, a good supper, and dancing for people from Santa Fe and Los Alamos. Oliver tried to dance me right into the floor. But we got them to our orchard where we sang, "Don't sit under the apple tree with anyone else but me..." The moon was full, the shadows deep. Oliver, a proper Bostonian by birth, did the Indian Hoop Dance for us in our driveway with all the expertise of an Indian.

We often went to El Nido, and we all danced then sat around a big table. I now have that table in my living room.

Oliver was responsible for our going one night to Alice Rossin's impromptu fiesta party. Alice was the ex-daughter-in-law of Mable Dodge Luhan. Mabel and her Taos Indian husband Tony and a group of Indians had stopped in at the party after a dance at the Santa Fe Plaza. The Indians had locked up their drums in the Governor's Palace before coming to Tesuque. Oliver knew we had an Indian ceremonial drum. A Tesuque Pueblo man had traded it to us for apples. Oliver asked us to come and bring our drum.

We joined Indians and Anglos dancing arm in arm in a circle by the light of an outside fire. Later, Tony, a big heavy Indian then sat in a canvas chair and told us something about Indian religious beliefs. While he was talking, the canvas gave way and dropped him to the ground. But he never missed a comma in his story.

Some time later, in Santa Fe, Tony was leaning against our wood-bodied station wagon waiting for us to finish grocery shopping. He wanted to buy our car. In those days most cars were either black or white, but we had painted ours orange-brown. I was ashamed of it but Tony wanted to buy it. Sted said, "no". I would have given it to him.

Sted once told friends that if I wanted someone for a tenant I would practically give them the house to get them to stay. One particular couple was Carrel and Bill Williams, both artists who had the same kind of background we had. They were from Chicago. The day they came looking for a house, I wasn't home. When Sted told me about them, I said, "Well, why didn't you rent the ranch house to them?"

"Because renting a house to people is your job."

He had asked Carrel and Bill to come back the next day when I would be home, after he had shown them the house and knew they wanted it. But he didn't even tell them how much the rent was.

Carrel and Bill told me they'd had visions of me as a big buxom woman, and couldn't have been more surprised when they saw me. I cut the rent for them that day, before they could have time to ask me how much it was, because I loved them. They told me that the house was so beautiful with the hollyhocks against the adobe walls that they were afraid to come back and see me for fear they couldn't afford it.

They had two boys about the same age as our boys, and we felt rich to have them. Bill was on a year's sabbatical from Batten, Barton, Durstine, and Osborn Advertising Agency. Our big studio was a favorite gathering spot for work and talk as always, or we took them to Indian dances and fiestas, July fireworks and Indian and Spanish Markets.

Marguerite McAdams, a Chicago concert pianist, was living in the little studio at the time Carrel and Bill came. Musicians are nice to have around. Piano compositions came floating through the apple blossoms as accompaniment to the sound of the irrigation water. It also served as a background as we were raking and burning the prunings.

The Vronsky and Babin team of pianists lived in the little studio house one summer. We had people stay a month, three months, a year. Some returned from time to time. A great many have made their homes in Santa Fe, as Irene did, and remained our fast friends.

Once we had a movie soundtrack composer named Daniele Amfitheatrof living in the Ranch House, and when he was home we heard just a few bars of music at a time. He would play them over and over, working the bugs out.

We had, long since the beginning experience with animals, succumbed to the idea that we should have a dog, then a cat, and following, two Toggenberg milk goats that each had two babies every spring. Tom had pigeons and ducks in a pond and then came the geese. I was the farmer and his wife with Tom my helper.

I remembered how the ladies of Bellaire used to whisper about women who whistled and pushed wheelbarrows. So far only one old woman had scoffed and wanted to know what my husband was doing while I was pushing the wheelbarrow. Carrel warned Bill not to get any ideas that she would ever work like I did.

Once she brought up the subject of parties. "Don't you remember how much it meant to you when you were a girl—which dress you should wear, which boy was to be your date, how excited and how prissy you were when you were just a little girl?"

"How little?" I asked.

"Why, from five on up," she said, and continued, "Of course, I wasn't allowed to go to a dance until I was sixteen, and then my mother went with me. But there were always parties and party dresses and boys."

"I missed all of that."

"Oh no, you couldn't have! Why, you missed the best time of your life!"

"I'm having the best time of my life right now," I told her.

"You mean, with all the responsibility of a husband, the ranch and the boys? Ugh, you can't mean that! However, I will say that you and Sted seem to enjoy your children more than any two people I ever knew. They're nice boys and I'm awfully fond of Sted, and so is Bill. We have a lot of fun here on the ranch but you just don't know what you missed if you didn't have a lot of fun when you were a girl!"

I didn't agree with her. There wasn't anything wrong with my girlhood. I had lived in a dream world and found one man who made all my dreams come true. This ranch community was Sted's idea; I never thought we'd be building our own community, but that's what it was.

I was enjoying a life comparable to the kind my parents and my older brothers and sister enjoyed when I was too little to do anything but look on. We made wonderful friends on the ranch, and we dreaded the day when any one of our tenants had to move away. We had our work and our friends, but the painting we wanted to do was too often pushed back for "more important things"—but too often for trivial things, too.

The days and weeks, months and years, rolled by. I learned something from everyone who lived on our place. Sometimes I learned the hard way; sometimes there were too many lessons, mostly those dealing with Sted. I was confused and baffled, and began to want a place to hide away where I could keep my beautiful belief in the goodness of my marriage and of humanity in general. I could never face a bad situation and do anything with it.

We read "Gone With The Wind" and saw the movie, and I felt a kindred spirit with Scarlett O'Hara. I amazed our friends one night when I told them I would like to be in life what she was. They protested, "Why, we couldn't imagine you flying off the handle like Vivien Leigh did in the movie."

"I must do my raging inside, then," I said. "Outwardly a Pollyanna. Inwardly? Well, who knows, maybe a Scarlett."

They just laughed at the idea. Wouldn't they be surprised if the tigress were let out of the cage just once instead of my keeping it locked up to chew my own insides?

"Do unto others as you would have them do unto you."

A meek little line from my mother's Bible quotes, but what a gag for me, stuffed tight in my throat until no words could get around it, my main thoughts hurting me instead of the other fellow. I would pussyfoot around and try to avoid trouble when my movements only helped trouble spot me.

I hated tears, my own tears, especially if Sted were the cause of them. Sted always said he was sorry and I mustn't mind, and he would sing:

> "Don't sigh and gaze at me,
> Your sighs are so like mine.
> Your eyes mustn't glow like mine,
> People will say we're in love..."

And what could I do but love him? Or what could I do but love a tenant when they didn't please me? If it eventually put things right between Sted and me, it should eventually put things right between friends. It seemed to work.

Sted was cross and at the same time too quiet of late. I didn't know what was in his mind and couldn't fathom him. It wasn't like him to sit quietly and not to work as he used to do. He was always able to perk up, though, when anyone would stop by to talk, and he was the life of the party when other artists and sculptors stopped by to see what we were doing. Sometimes, we would have life drawing sessions or just sit and talk art and show whatever new stuff we had to show.

Sted had been doing The New Mexico Magazine illustrations every month, selling a painting once in a while, and doing art work for the New Mexico Tourist Bureau. Some of his work was published in national magazines. I helped him with illustrative work from time to time, just like in the old studio days in Houston.

His painting ability was recognized. Randall Davey wantèd to sponsor him for membership in something of national importance, but he didn't want to be bothered about all the crating and shipping and headaches that would entail. So he continued in the pattern of independence that he'd cut out for himself as an illustrator first and a painter second. He was invited to give talks and to judge shows, but he turned it all down.

I taught an art class at the Loretto Academy in Santa Fe one year, and exhibited the class work afterwards at the Fine Arts Museum of New Mexico. My own work was well received. People were always asking me about my painting. I painted to please myself and people could feel that in them and liked what the paintings made them feel.

My letters to people who had lived on the ranch were enthusiastically received and joyfully answered. On the other hand, letters to and from Sted concerned more serious worldly matters.

Chapter 12

Sted had been following the threat of war. "In spite of what Roosevelt says, we'll soon be in another world war. It's inevitable."

"Why is it inevitable? It's unconstitutional to enter into foreign wars. Why can't we mind our own business and keep out of it? What did we get for doing all we did in the last world war? We didn't get any thanks for it or get back the money we loaned. The other countries just thumbed their noses at us."

"That's true," he said. "But the world has changed. We have many interests in Europe and our trade is affected."

"But we could get along without their trade for a while and be in less trouble than if we went into another war. If we have interests over there, are they national or individual interests? How does it happen that we have interests in foreign lands that jeopardize the whole nation?"

"Well, there are a lot of things you don't know."

"I can't follow it like you do. Tell me what's going on."

"It wouldn't do any good if I did because you don't see it the way I do."

"Those of you who fought in the first war have changed your feelings about another war, too. How often have I heard you say that you would never fight again?"

"I'm telling you that things have changed. Hitler is out to conquer the world."

"If and when he does, I'll fight to protect my own home and homeland. But I don't think he'll get that far."

"He's like wildfire—the more he gains, the harder he'll be to stop. We should have been in before now to stop him."

"Maybe you're right. But I hate the drum-beating and the song-singing that make young men's blood rush into joining up. My blood stands still. I remember the first world war."

"You were too little to worry."

"I was just at the age when it couldn't have affected me more deeply. And besides, I had you to worry about, didn't I?"

"You did not!"

"I did so."

"Did you do any praying for me?"

"Every night and between times."

Then came the Pearl Harbor incident. And at the same time, Sted's father died in Houston, and he went immediately to be with his mother and brothers and sister. He wrote to me about moving back to Houston, maybe to stay. The war, he said, would affect our renting for a long time.

I didn't want to sell and move and go through all the upheaval again, but he had the itch and that's what had been bothering him. He had never lived more than five years in one place. Soon, we'd have been here ten years. We had done all that we had set out to do; now do you suppose he has to move on to someplace else, war or no war? If so, wouldn't it be better to keep what we had and buy another piece of property close by? I thought of the old nursery we had wanted in the first place. If we bought that, it would give Sted something to work on for another ten years and still be close enough to look after this place. Just move downstream a bit, as it were. Not way off to the gulf.

Sted came back from Houston and no sooner got back than Kruger and Associated Architects phoned him and wanted him to work at Los Alamos for the War Department. It would be helping with the war in our own backyard. He would be able to get home twice a week to see us.

We were feeling the closeness of this place that we had built up and it would be fun to start something new while the boys were young enough to help us do it. We had known for ten years that the nursery was for sale and that the owners, our friends the Callins, had always wanted us to buy it. There was money in the bank, and where could one put accumulated money more safely than in land?

But Sted wasn't sure he wanted more land. He said he had a feeling that the land would own him instead of him owning the land. Above all, he didn't want to farm.

But Tom and I had been idly dreaming of the nursery for two years. It was half a mile north of us; a long twenty acre piece of land lying between the Big Tesuque River running the full length on the west and the highway to the east. There was a high pinon-covered ridge and sheer bluff on the far side of the river and three long ponds fed by springs along the river.

A German-American had built the ponds and stocked them with fish. There were boats in which his friends and patrons floated lazily around under the big weeping willows which trailed and dipped their tresses into the pond, making perfect secret hiding places for lovers.

During the week his mill, at the south end of the first pool, ground corn for his neighbors; and on Sundays and holidays he served fried chicken and fish on big tables in the orchard and under the cottonwood trees. To the east, on the other side of the highway, lay a strip of valley, then red voluptuous foothills with their patterned print of pinon and beyond that, more rugged mountains and valleys leading into the Sangre de Cristo Mountains, and above them the vast impressive sky which gave me perspective on—and compassion for—my own predicament as well as the war.

I love the sky.

Sometimes it feels calm and is of the purest blue, and when it's angry it's black and thunderous with jagged sharpness. Sometimes it feels expansive, with its big round puffy moist clouds. A proud and mighty man might look up and swell his chest and say the sky is a mirror reflecting his emotions. A meek or humble man would look up and say the sky feels as he does today too.

The nodding of the trees, the whispering of the grass, and the silence of the earth seem to side with the humble man, but the mighty man is right, too. In him is a spark of that creative power; will he use it creatively or will he just bluster and blow? Will he be a peacemaker or a warrior?

Feeling, impulse, desire and will lead to creative action. A vast mass of people can be slow-moving and refuse to be rushed into action, a check-rein to either a good or evil deed; or people can act as one in accord to promote either good or evil. They are like the sun and the rain on the seed in the ground. They are the force that makes the seed grow.

My sons tell me that one seedling drop of moisture turns to hail before the whole cloud turns into the hail which will destroy our crops; or one bit of seedling moisture turns into a raindrop before the whole cloud turns from floating vapor to life-giving waters which will fall and quench the thirst of the earth. Whether masses of people or masses of clouds, it takes just one seedling idea to start action. There is the same pattern of behavior in man and nature.

I thought of these things as I walked down to the nursery and I thought to myself: it's such a wonderful thrill to come out from under the canopy of tree branches and leaves and see only the sky when one has been too long in the shade.

I had forgotten about this on our place because I worked outside so much and looked up whenever there was a tiny patch of sky to be seen. That whole sky that was above me, as I walked in the openings between the rows of flowers at the nursery or walked through the grass in the sun, made me feel as though I'd been in the dark about many things; been too long reflecting on old matters. I felt as though the sun from the open sky was pouring new ideas and courage into me, making me want to do things.

A terrific desire was building up in me. To paint? No...maybe next winter or next summer, but not now. I wanted to plant alfalfa and build more fences, another house and barn, new roads and gateways; a house stretched out in the sun like a lizard, with big windows for the sun and light to come in, through which we could look to the mountains and to the river or to the cottonwoods at either end of the place.

"Oh, Sted, don't we have just one more house in our system? I have. It's something like my idea which had a stillbirth on paper before we built the Big House."

This nursery is the place of my dreams, I thought to myself. It has everything—trees and open space, the river and mountains and peace and quiet. If I could only get Sted wanting to own this place. "Oh dear God, why does he just sit and look at nothing when he's home these days? Why doesn't he do things like he used to? Why doesn't he smile and laugh and sing like he used to? Is it a feeling of insecurity due to the war? Is he grieving over his dad? Is it me?"

"It isn't you," I heard as I walked along the river back toward home.

"It isn't?"

"If he blames you, it's because he doesn't know himself."

"But he shuts up like a clam when I say 'let's do something,' or he does it without heart, whatever it is—whether it's a movie, friends, or anything."

The voice continued, "But he's done so much. Sometimes people have to pause and look back and questions their actions; to make up their minds that they've been going in the right direction."

I said, "Joaquin, the old one-eyed Spanish man, has been telling me that Mr. Stedman will get sick working inside so much. Do you think it would help if he could be outside more? If he came out in the sunshine, would he feel better?"

"The sun brings courage and strength and new ideas out like it brings the bud out in spring."

Listening to myself or whatever and arguing this way was an old habit with me.

"If only I had learned to finesse when we used to play bridge—but I never liked card games."

"Because you were never good at it."

"No, you're wrong!" I said. "I wasn't good at it because I didn't like it. But I wish I had learned to finesse. When I really want something, I want it too much to play tricks, though."

"Don't kid yourself," scoffed the voice. "You can scheme and plan and finesse better than anyone I know."

"Thanks. But it's really not satisfying. That's why I don't get much pleasure out of some things. A little while after I get them, my conscience hurts me."

"Stuff and fiddlesticks! I don't see that you've been walking over anybody. You have to know you're right and then go after it. Sted isn't going to let you make him do anything he doesn't really want to do. Now...on Sunday just suggest a walk. Pretend you don't care which direction you walk in, but if he wants to go down past the nursery way, it's kind of nice down here along the river and then up through the nursery for a look at the mountains."

"This doesn't sound right. It sounds like some scheming nincompoop! I'm going to forget all about the whole thing."

"You can't do that. Where do you think the idea came from in the first place?"

The plan was reviewed:

"You have money in the bank. What if the banks go broke like they did in the thirties? The money isn't earning you anything in your checking account. Buy this place, rent the Big House, live in the thirty-foot adobe potting shed at the nursery, and build the house as you can. It will be something to do, and something for the boys to do. You will all love it and work together for it; and it will mean more peace and happiness to you, more freedom to work on something worthwhile after you get settled. It's a new goal. All you need is the courage of your convictions."

"Then you don't think I'm crying for the moon?"

"The moon prompts feelings and reflections. You've had time for all that. What you have now is the sun in your lap. The seed is planted, the sun is warm. Keep the idea warm and watch it grow."

"That's a tall order."

It came back with, "Nothing ventured, nothing gained. Good luck, kid—and too-da-loo, snapoo, goodbye-eyee..."

I quickened my pace, because I realized it was getting close to suppertime, but the voice came back again:

"Don't you think you've been reflecting too long about your folks? Don't you think it's time you did something about that, too?"

"You know I have started to do something about it several times, only to be slapped down again by some letter or comment from someone in Houston."

"You're just afraid. Take the bull by the horns and go see them. This would be an excellent time. You have to work fast on this real estate deal, though."

"Oh, be off with you!"

"Too-da-loo."

———

Sted was the one who needed a vacation. He needed to get away for a while so that he could look back on what he'd done, and realize that he really didn't need to worry about small things the way he did—that in the whole we had accomplished so much and reached a point that, singly, neither of us would have attained. We were now coasting along when we needed to work. That was my way of looking at our situation. If we looked at the war as Sted was doing, wouldn't it be a good idea for the boys and me to be raising some food for ourselves and the animals? We had to do something with our money and time that would stabilize our security in this rocking old world.

Everyone I knew was tense and wondering what they should be doing. I rolled bandages and worked with the Red Cross once a week along with other women of the neighborhood.

But if I went away to see my parents, it would give Sted a chance to make up his mind about me: whether I was important to him, or if he'd rather I stayed away and left him alone to do exactly as he pleased. He could put the pots and pans where he liked, clean out all the closets and the basement, cook what he liked and cook it the way he wanted, shop and buy the way he thought it should be done.

These were the things he complained about. He was a homebody at heart, but the way he worried you'd think he hated it. I was a homebody, too, and really liked doing all the things that went with that, and got a tremendous thrill from it all—if my mind could go places while my hands took care of all the detail and routine. If I had to fasten my mind down, the task would become only dull routine.

Everything I did must be touched with romance. If I cleaned up the kitchen, I cleaned it to see it sparkle, not because it needed it. And I'd do it when I was in the spirit. Most of the time it did sparkle, but somehow Sted always managed to see that it needed a cleaning ahead of me and just made it plain work by calling it to my attention.

How could a man be so concerned over such things? He had to have a lot of mother instinct in him. He felt the need to protect and care for everything he owned. Nothing was too small or insignificant for his attention. I told myself that was a wonderful trait, but at the same time I wanted to tell him to mind his own business. Instead, I trained myself to anticipate his moods and work accordingly. He felt it was his business since he was the master of the house, and I would only have a war on my hands if I complained. He was serious about everything these days.

He didn't want to buy the nursery because he'd feel that he would personally have to get around to all the trees and shrubs and see that they were pruned and watered; to see that nature didn't take them over. This was the same man who so admired the natural beauty of the mountain meadows and the Canadian woods. I didn't realize that he would try to take all these things out of nature's hands. That would be a job.

After he told me all the reasons he didn't want to buy the place I was thoroughly through with the matter and had personally called the Callins and definitely told them the deal was off. Up to this point he didn't even know the price and when he did, out of curiosity, he began to enumerate all the reasons he now wanted to buy the place and in two days made the announcment: "Well, Mrs. Stedman, I've bought you a ranch." What a man! 1943.

He told me to go along and see my folks and get things fixed up there, which I did, much to everyone's satisfaction. While I was away, I received a wonderful letter from him that would warm the coldest heart. When I got home the house was fairly dirty, and I had the feeling that the house and my three men had missed me. They seemed to love me in spite of all my faults and idiosyncracies, and I'd have to store that in my mind to tide me over the bad times when there were scorning criticisms in Sted's eyes and try to understand how these things and love could go together without destroying something.

Maybe I should take another lesson from the sky. The sky could darken, flash lightning—and in a few hours could act as though nothing ever happened. Why couldn't I do the same? Why did I have to retain the thunder and hurt? Why couldn't I realize it was good to roar and be roared at once in a while? I couldn't realize it because I wasn't brought up that way. Could I learn to take it and like it? The sky always managed to look cleaner, calmer, and more beautiful after a storm. Why couldn't I? We'd see.

Whether I told Sted or not, I always figured it was me who was wrong in not being able to hold him in mind as that immaculate conception that all men of God's making really are. After just a moment of thinking this way, I could look at him and see his eyes soften. They focused on mine and melted right in if I turned to look at him for an instant.

My spirits were lifted too by a chance remark at William Penhallow Henderson's funeral service held at his daughter Alice's house in Tesuque in 1943. Randall Davey was there. He told Tom, "You have a very talented mother." This from him was just what I needed.

This "Whippy," as William Henderson was affectionately called, was one of the first of the Santa Fe artists to die since we arrived. An Indian blanket, his big Western hat, and a cane topped the casket. Friends toasted his memory by joining in on a feast and engaging in lively conversation. This, too, impressed me in a wonderful way. It was good to get out of my own shadow.

CHAPTER 13

The news that we had bought the nursery spread fast: "They must have a system worth knowing about. Where did they get the money to buy one of the nicest pieces of property in the whole valley? They didn't get that piece for a song."

Sted began to feel good again. I think he felt good the minute he made up his mind to buy it. Everyone told him what a nice piece he'd bought, and they wondered how he did it.

He did it by pruning his expenses and watering his income. He never overlooked a thing or spared himself. If he hadn't always been that way, we wouldn't have the place. Every little bit helps—work, string, time or money. I don't think Sted ever threw anything away or let a thing fall apart for want of a little attention.

We often laughed because he sometimes said, "You know how long I've had this razor? Thirty years ago I bought it in Winnipeg, and I've used it ever since." Or he would say, "You know where that old iron chest came from? It came over with us from England when I was eleven."

I could see the family picture: Sted's father, a prosperous-looking young businessman with a top hat, spats and cane; his mother was trim and dressy with quick blue eyes, a light step, and hearty laughter for one so small. His dad wasn't more than an inch or two taller than his mother, but when he walked along swinging his cane and humming a tune everyone said, "Good morning, Thomas."

Or if he was among people who didn't know him, they spoke because he looked like someone they thought they ought to know. He walked as though he owned the ground he walked on. He had often been wealthy and often broke. Every time he got ahead he sank his money into the business, always expanding until it sometimes would get out of hand, or he invested in stock and sometimes diamonds.

Sted's mother always had money, sometimes several hundred in the teapot, saved from her weekly allowance for the house. She never knew if Thomas had any money or if he didn't. He kept his business to himself. He often made the statement that he would, "never leave any money for his sons to play ducks and drakes with."

So that is how it was on Sted's side; anything he got he knew he would have to earn. But he had his mother's frugality.

On my side, my father used to tell his friends: "Just anything you need, speak up. If we have it and you need it, it's yours." Though we never had very much.

Sometimes I would see my mother hunt for days for a certain article, and sooner or later come out with, "Land o' livin', I believe I gave that to Norma last year when she and Albert were having such a hard time. Or did I give it to Minnie when her baby came? I think I gave it to Norma, and I bet two cents she didn't need it half as bad as I do now."

"Well, why do you give everything away?" I asked. "You'll give the shirt off your back and think so little of it that you forget you gave it and who you gave it to. You're too generous for your own good."

"Oh well, I thought she needed it worse than I did at the time, and I don't really need it now. Just thought I'd use it if it were still around."

A chip off her father's block. He was a cooper who would always invite his customers to stay for dinner.

So my inheritance from my father and mother would be a few old tin-types they knew I loved, a small gold watch with fine engravings, and a lot of kind and friendly traits. I treasured it all.

What Sted and I had was due to our own efforts. That was true, but there was more truth that went with it. There was this: "All good gifts are from above."

What was this "above"?

Sted said, "Answers aren't going to come out of space from the throat of a long-bearded being in the sky, or presents either."

"I have no such picture of God. God to me is an expressive and receptive Mind," I heard myself saying for the first time even to myself. "All gifts are of this Mind."

Mind spelled with a capital "M" could be God or infinity but infinity would include the tiniest speck of intelligence. Seen this way, Mind could be also Mind spelled with a little "m", ever present in us.

"Everything is spiritual."

"You're a funny one to be talking like that, what about all the material things you want?"

"The material things are just the things that the Mind has already given us; there's lots more where they came from, made of the same stuff."

"I thought I gave you all the things you have."

"You did—through using your mind. Mind is our biggest inheritance and our truest investment. Everything we have is a good investment, an investment in Mind, however you want to spell it."

"Tell that to a banker and see how much money he'll loan you on it. And it won't be a good investment to build one house in the middle of twenty acres. Any banker will tell you that, too."

"But the land is an investment that will increase in value. You don't have to do anything with it. It will be an ace in the hand for the boys to do something with after we are through with it."

"I just hate tying money up in something that will take years to get a return on. It'll take five years before I can get up enough money to build a house on that property."

"You can start getting a return on your investment next spring."

"How have you got that figured out?"

"We can move down into the little adobe house that's on the place and rent the Big House, and I'll prove to you that I can be happy with very little."

"You couldn't live down there. Why, it's only one room! There's no water, no electricity, no gas, no telephone. Uh-uh. I've already bought the place, you know, so you don't have to say these things to get me to buy it."

"I know," I laughed, "but you'll be away most of the time up at Los Alamos, and I want to live down there in that little house through the summer. The boys have a tent and bedrolls; they can sleep in the tent or under a tree and I can fix the house up as cute as a bug's ear."

"I'll get an old wood stove to cook on. We can haul our water, take our baths in the river, and go to bed when the light fails. I can't wait to live down there on that place. Also, I want to get something coming in for your investment, and by having the Big House rented we can figure we're doing that."

He just looked at me with sparkles in his eyes which approved my idea—and thus it became his idea.

"You're one in a million," he told me. "We'll call this place the Cottonwoods."

CHAPTER 14

We moved straggling rows of nursery stock from the two-acre patch that was between the location we'd chosen for the house and the highway. In this space I wanted to plant oats and alfalfa. It should look like a large green lawn and give us lots of feed for the Toggenburg goats and horses, and wouldn't obstruct our view of the mountains.

I could close my eyes and imagine how that field would look with the wind sweeping over it in long lazy swirls. I could remember the same thing happening in the tall thick prairie grass on the flat plains all around Bellaire where I lived as a child.

Corn had been planted in part of this space and the stalks had never been cut so we cut them and stacked them for the goats to eat. We should have disked it into the land but we couldn't find anyone with a disker.

Sometimes, it was warm and mellow, the sort of spring day that makes the ground loose and fluffy. When it was cold we roasted wieners over our fires, warmed up a pot of beans and a pot of coffee, and ate our lunch while we rested and warmed ourselves. When the day was warm we picnicked under the trees at lunchtime. Once or twice we took potatoes and hamburgers down by the ponds and Carrel and Bill and their two boys ate a picnic supper there with us until the cool dusk came.

When Sted wasn't with us, because of his work at Los Alamos, the boys and I got the ground ready for seed with the help of the New Mexico Soil Conservation Program for helping landowners with such projects, and this was with big equipment. Tom operated the equipment and did a good job under their direction.

Tom said, "I'm going to have a thousand acres somewhere up in the mountains, and a lot of machinery to operate and keep in shape."

"Is it the machinery you like, Tom, or the farming?" I asked.

"I like both. I like to see things growing. I would like to stand and look over a lot of land that's mine, to see a big shed of all kinds of machinery. I'd like to have a big plant on the place where I could manufacture the machinery myself, and have the farm where machinery could be tried out. I could work the bugs out of the equipment before it went on the market."

I told him, "When I was a little girl in school, we had a teacher who said she could see stars in our eyes. She said it was the reflection of the stars we hitched our wagons to. She used me as a demonstration for the class because my eyes were big and black. I've looked for stars in people's eyes all my life. Your eyes are like mine. There are stars in your father's eyes, and in Wilfred's, too."

"Did you have your wagon hitched to a star?"

"My mother hitched me up to a star by wanting me to be an artist. I stayed in the seat. She also wanted me to marry an artist, long before I met your father. It's funny how I can look back and see in dreams how everything was always there ahead of its appearance."

"And what happens now that your dream has become a reality?" Tom wanted to know.

"Oh, well, a dream is like life itself. It just goes on and on. The high pitch of my dream is to have all these things in a beautiful place where I can contemplate and study, as well as be a part of things going on in and around me."

"This is a beautiful place. But what about Daddy? Do you think he loves this place like we do? Is it a part of his dream?"

"He told me that he's always loved the country. When he was a boy in England he roamed the country and the seaside; when he was in an architectural office in Canada he commuted to a place in the woods; when he lived in Wisconsin he painted with a friend around the lakes and country; he loved the country in France; and when we came out here he didn't want to live in Santa Fe. Yes, he told me he wanted to live in a little valley just north of Santa Fe. And this is the place he wanted in the beginning."

We rented the Big House and the day we moved into the one-room adobe I was worn out and dubious about the whole thing. Sted was at Los Alamos that day so the boys and I had our first breakfast cooked outside the door on a camp grate because we didn't as yet have our smoke pipe up on our wood stove.

The boys thought it was great fun. We couldn't back out, anyway, because the other people were in our house with the rent paid, so Tom and I connected the stove pipe up to the stove and made a hole through the adobe wall for the pipe to go through. I got my plaid curtains up, some of Sted's pen-and-ink drawings on the walls, books on the bookshelves, and some flowers in a vase and felt better.

The boys helped and were in and out like a couple of bees. They were setting up their tent, and and it was like being in a beautiful spot miles and miles from everyone on a camping trip. Soon the little house shaped up and responded to my decorating job better than anything I'd ever done.

I had planned carefully and had everything we needed—a long table to prepare food on with the water bucket sitting at one end and a washbasin and mirror at the other end behind the opened door; the old wood stove that was a nice-looking old thing with a high back and warming oven up above; a nine-foot-long pine cupboard with closed doors for food and dishes, pots and pans and, on top at one end of it, two shelves for pretties, a big Mexican platter, blue glassware bottles, a clock, a lamp, and a small painted Mexican chest full of needles and thread.

We had a pine dining table and chairs, two studio beds that were also couches, an end table, an easy chair, two chests of drawers, two wooden blanket chests, a big Mexican basket, and Sted's big drawing table. A brown woven rug and Indian rugs covered a tamped-earth floor. The bookcase was built into a closed-up doorway in one wall. The opposite wall was all beautiful windows. One end of the room also had a long high window.

We had lots of cool days and nights that summer, so the old wood stove felt good crackling and clanging, and gave the place an aroma from the applewood smoke. Kerosene lamps hung on the walls, and candles were in brown Mexican pottery holders. Ash trays were alongside Mexican cups which held matches. Just outside the door was a low adobe wall where we put a water barrel with a tap spigot on it and some potted geraniums. The water barrel was immortalized in one of Theodore Van Soelden's Western lithographs. An apricot tree grew in a small patio formed by the house and the wall. Beneath the tree were a table and some outdoor chairs I made.

The boys had two army cots, a table and stool in the tent, and a place to hang a lantern. The goats were housed in a little corral, partly roofed over, and there were cedar posts on two sides for a windbreak and shelter. The ducks and geese were in their big pond enclosures down by the river, and the two horses had the run of the old apple orchard. The coyotes ganged up and made a terrific racket with their yapping and crying at night, and one night a wolf howled just a few feet away.

The boys poofed at my fright and stuck to their tent. Many nights Tom slept in a bedroll out somewhere. I never knew just where until he answered my call in the morning. Lucky, the dog, always slept with him. One night it began to thunder and lightning, and Lucky crawled into the bedroll clear down to the foot. Tom came in the next morning, soaking wet but laughing.

He said, "Lucky loosened the snaps and the water got into the bed."

"And you slept all night in that water?"

"Yeah, after a while the water got warm and I went back to sleep."

Lucky had the sense to keep absolutely quiet and out of the way of the coyotes. I noticed that all the dogs in this end of the valley barked when the coyotes were far away but didn't make a sound if they were close. A few times during the day we saw one or two in the orchard, and then if you blinked your eyes they were gone like a shadow.

We had a heavy rain once a week most all summer long. The oats and alfalfa got a good start and waved in the breeze. We cut it and got it stacked for feed between rains. Sometimes at night I had occasion to be out away from the house with a slicker and a lantern, and when I looked back at the little house I knew the boys were sitting in there at the tables playing dominoes, or on couches reading a book. Sometimes, Sted was with them, because he came in from Los Alamos on Wednesday evenings and then on Saturday nights for the weekends. Our voices, the rain, or the little flickering noise the lamps sometimes made and the fire crackling were the only things to break the quiet.

I was so glad that we had no radio and no telephone. We all did a lot more reading and a lot more family talking, joking, and planning; and a lot more sleeping and resting. It was a lazy summer.

Tom dug the foundations for a shop. I helped him build wooden forms, and we got the foundations poured. He worked on fences and did something each day, but spent a good portion of the day reading. I put up some jam and went for my daily plunge in two feet of cold river water on sunny days.

There were a lot of snakes on the place, and I was never certain about them. We had books from the library and colored charts on the wall picturing poisonous and non-poisonous snakes.

One day, I was just outside the house cutting some weeds with a hoe when I noticed a big snake stretched out in the sun. My first inclination was to chop it in two with my hoe and look it up afterwards but as it started to move to hide under some logs, I set the hoe down gently but firmly on its head, pinning it to the ground.

I called for Wilfred to bring me the colored chart. We looked it up and found the snake to be a friend, so I lifted my hoe and let him go. In a month or so there weren't many snakes around, though, because the geese were there. Some people would prefer the snakes to the geese, but I loved our geese. They always told me when there was anyone coming.

We could go for days on end without seeing anyone but ourselves, and then we'd have a picnic supper and see our whole bunch of friends. If I had been worried for a second about what people would say about our living in a one-room house, I needn't have been.

Sted sometimes came home cranky and cross and complained about this and that: because the boys hadn't done anything he'd asked them to do. I had to assure him that the boys thought he was okay, and assure the boys that he was okay—and I had to watch my own step, only to fall in an unsuspected trap because I didn't know what the real trouble was.

I thought he was worried about buying the place, so I talked to the boys and told them their father was worried, and I was afraid it was because we had this place. I asked how they would feel if he wanted to sell it, and they both put up a big fuss. So I told them they would have to help us and show their father that they loved the place and were helping.

I asked Sted if he was sorry we had the place and he said, "No, I'm not sorry. What makes you think that?"

"Well, then, are you sorry we're living down here in this little house?"

"No. That's the smart thing to do."

So that wasn't it either.

Then it dawned on me that working at Los Alamos was getting to him, as I'd heard a lot of people complaining of the tension, the secrecy, the security guards, the confinement and the uncertainty as to what the War Department was doing. The drafting Sted did was so segmented that he hadn't the slightest idea what any of the overall plans might look like except in the beginning when they'd been working on the fast and temporary housing projects for the people who had to live up there.

When the War Department took over the area, the only thing up in that isolated mountain area was a big log lodge which was a boys' school. It was a beautiful twenty-eight mile drive from Tesuque, which Sted enjoyed except for the speed with which the car-pool driver took the hairpin turns.

Sted had always admitted that he didn't like working for anyone else. Now I knew he was getting anxious to get on with his own art work and the building of our house.

———

As summer ended, the boys and I moved to the Little Studio House. The Barettos, who had the Big House, wanted to stay on through the winter. He wrote stories for national magazines and she had something to do with the collection of paintings for the Library of Congress.

Roul Tunley, also a writer and the editor of a popular women's magazine, was their guest. They liked my watercolors, and Mrs. Baretto took some back to New York—she said she considered me one of the best of the Santa Fe artists. The watercolors were liked very much in New York, but I didn't produce enough to establish a lasting contact. However, I did a lot of painting that winter.

When Sted was at home he worked around the grounds and on plans for our new house. He told Carrel and Bill that he was going to let me help plan this one. But, we both planned and lived with our plans until we got ideas for changes. Sted was sometimes annoyed and wanted to hold to certain things.

"Just to have something settled."

"But we won't be building it for a long time yet, so why not keep thinking about it and making changes until we have it just exactly like we'll want it?"

"I keep on making detailed drawings, and then you come along and upset it all."

"Well, stop making detailed drawings and let's make rough sketches until it's like we want it."

For several days there was a strained feeling between us, and then, almost simultaneously, we began to hit on the idea that while the basic plan was beginning to shape up into the type of house we wanted, we could simplify it which is what I was getting at.

When the first of June came, we moved back to the little adobe—Sted with us this time, because he'd quit the war work. He wanted to get the new house started—not to be built all at once, but just a section; he wanted to get the roof on and the doors and windows in.

Our friends couldn't believe that Sted and Tom were really going to start building all by themselves. They knew that Sted could design houses, but didn't know he could do the actual work. Tom was just sixteen, but he was strong and willing. Sted was amazed at the way he could work, and at the way he understood what was to be done. Sted made sketches of the different points of the work as they came to them, showing Tom what was to be done and how, and Tom followed it all with amazing intelligence and worked side by side with Sted, or by himself like an experienced builder.

In the beginning, Sted had told me that it was my job to see that they got enough to eat. "That's your first job."

So I said, "All right, I'll make it my first and most important." But I knew that I'd be doing all of the buying and a thousand and one things.

The cook stove and everything was in place as it had been the first summer, but this time we had a well in the backyard so we didn't have to haul water. It was little Wilfred's first and most important job to see that there was wood for the stove. He had to scout around and cut it wherever he could find it on the place, saw it up, and get it into the wood box. He was only twelve, so on occasion I had to encourage or browbeat him at his job. He wanted to help with the house, doing something really important, but always got assigned to picking up the scrap ends of lumber.

"Why don't you get some fresh kidneys today when you go to town so you can make a beefsteak and kidney pie for supper?"

Tom said, "And bring home some fish for lunch. I could eat fish three times a day! Daddy likes fish, too, so don't forget to give us fish often. And jello, and cheese for macaroni—and make us some good bread like you make...mmm."

We all liked food, and each of us liked certain things. We all ate the same thing for a meal, but I would favor one and then the other, and I enjoyed cooking for them because they always had good appetites. Sted liked all the dishes his mother used to cook, such as knuckle of veal or shin of beef, soups with barley, kidney, liver and onions, heart, tripe, fresh pig's feet, mutton stew, and lots of fish.

Once in a while he liked rare beef roast or a pot roast with carrots, onions, and potatoes, or a thick juicy steak, and he liked stewed chicken and chicken pot pie. I learned to make onion soup and a pie crust that would melt in your mouth.

There was wild asparagus growing on the place, and lamb's-quarters (which is like spinach but with a much milder flavor); tender dandelion leaves and a little alfalfa were good in salads.

There were raspberries and black currants, apricots, apples, pears, and, at the end of the season, grapes on the place and fresh mint for drinks and sauce for lamb or mutton roast. We had roast duck from our own pond, and a young goose once in a while. I could cook all these things just the way they liked them.

Sted was now singing all the old songs and a lot that I had never heard before. Tom laughed and sang, too, and you could always expect an unexpected comment with a bit of humor. They were real pals. Sted seemed happier than he had ever been. He had a world of endurance, too. Sometimes I would stand at the door waiting to call him to lunch, and he would be sawing off a round viga end, and I might stand there for ten minutes waiting for him to pause in his sawing so he could hear me.

If he were having difficulty with the work he might come in to lunch with a nervous sniffling and wouldn't be hungry or wouldn't like what I had for lunch or how it was cooked. Instead of resting after lunch he'd be right out at the work, and wouldn't stop or let up until he had the difficulty licked.

There would be tension in the air that kept us all tiptoeing around until we'd hear Sted start to sing or hear him laughing. Sometimes Tom could break up the tension by lending his wit or strength to the problem. For the greater part of the time, things were smoother and happier than they had been for two years.

Around four o'clock everybody stopped working and went down to the Indian dam for a swim. People from our other ranch sometimes came down around that time to go swimming with them. Sometimes it would look like we were having a party by the number of cars parked in the turnaround. They brought their own beer. We would all have one, and snacks, before they went home.

In the evening we sat under the apricot tree and watched the clouds in the sky, the color changing on the mountains, and the moon riding through the clouds. Or we lounged around reading magazines and books, played dominoes or checkers, or visited with our closest friends.

Fall came and we had to move back to the other place to take care of the fruit. We left the ducks and geese, because I wanted to continue to come down for just a little while each day. One morning when I was feeding the ducks, Lucky was excitedly sniffing around the grapevines. I found the grass trampled down around them and most of the grapes gone. There in the mud was a big bear track, and another track or two up by the little house. I hurried home and told one-eyed Joaquin, who was picking fruit.

He said another man had seen three bears on the ranch just across and down the river from ours. He said they had come down out of the mountains looking for fruit because there were no berries or nuts in the mountains this year. He told me I better go back and get my goats.

When the boys went back after the ducks and geese that evening, they found two Indian calves in a corner of the old orchard by the ducks' pen. One was dead and the other lay with its back broken. The mother cows stood over them sniffing and mooing softly. After that we left the place to the bears, but in a day or two a neighbor shot one bear and said two more took off to the mountains.

Every time there was a lull in our emotional life my thoughts turned to a growing obsession, a search for things unknown. I could feel the scientific intelligence gathered at Los Alamos buzzing around my head.

Tantalizing!

It was about this time that I started writing "Of One Mind." It came like poetry in the night with more meaning than I was capable of understanding.

CHAPTER 15

The tornado was a quick flash of temper, as freakish as the strong twist of wind that brought it on. Tom and I were working under some cottonwood trees over by the goat pen, stacking hay in a rush because the sky was black with a rain cloud coming toward us fast. We had been working with alfalfa for three days.

Two stacks were left in the field under tarps. If we could get the remaining hay off the trailer and into the haybarn before the rain hit, none of it would get wet. We began to hear a roaring sound, and saw a twister come down the river and up the bank, hurling trees all around us.

There was a loud bang, and then another. I looked straight up above us and saw the whole upper part of a large cottonwood tree jump in the air, crash into an adjoining tree, and both of them were coming down over our heads. Tom was looking in another direction.

I threw myself against him and screamed for him to run. The top end branches caught me and knocked me down, knocked my Stetson hat off and sent it flying thirty feet. Sted had been working on the roof of the house but he scrambled down and by the time I was up on my feet like a cat he was there with his face in mine, screaming mad, shouting that if we'd had the alfalfa in before now this wouldn't have happened.

His face was too close. I hauled off and slapped him hard.

He looked startled, then red, and said, "No one can slap me and get away with it." And he slapped me back.

It had all happened in a split second, and yet it seemed to have a slow-motion quality to it.

I shouted, "We've been working on haying all day and some the day before and the day before that!"

He walked back to the house. Young Wilfred was standing by me and the wind was blowing. Things were flying. I looked to see where Tom had gone. He was out in the field trying to put the tarp back on a stack of hay.

I asked Wilfred, "Did Tom see that?"

"No, I don't think so."

"Don't say anything to him about it."

I glanced at those two heavy green cottonwood trees that had smashed down where we'd been standing, and then walked to the house. Sted was by the side of the house pulling up weeds. When I got close, he raised up with, "How do you do, Mrs. Stedman?"

I grinned at him. "How do you do yourself, Mr. Stedman?"

While we ate supper that evening, there was hardly a word spoken. Afterwards Sted was sitting out under the apricot tree; I was inside washing dishes. I looked through the window above my dish pan at him, and he looked at me with a look that I could have painted but I don't think I could describe.

He had no more control over his temper than the clouds had in the face of the wind and he knew it. It was as though the wind had become his temper, which meant to strike us down. Why, of all the trees on the place, did those two come down? Why was he there so quickly?

I was ready to give the whole thing up and go back to the city, to an apartment where we wouldn't even have a tree, but for that look of his through the window, I could see that the storm was over.

Should life be all harmonious and peaceful, or like a symphony— full of discord and clashes set together in a balance of harmony? I attached too much importance to the clashes and let them throw me off balance. There had never been a dull moment in our lives together, and I suspected that Sted's life would have been a whole lot quieter if it were not for me. I felt purged of some sin, for insisting on planting the alfalfa, for having this place, for anything I might have done that I shouldn't have.

Sted followed impulses that I didn't feel. He was bombastic, but he was a doer. He got things done in no sketchy way. He had a way of building up a wall of reserve around himself while he worked, so that no one could interfere or say "boo." He had resented the interference the alfalfa caused, of Tom helping me instead of him on the house, then the sudden fear that all would have stopped if Tom and I had been killed by those trees.

It was my nature to skip along ahead and over all of the detail and do a lot of dreaming. I knew Sted was good for me, and I thought I was good for him. My dreaming got him into jobs, but sometimes I couldn't even recognize them as my ideas after they were carried out, because of how he did them.

But he always said, "I've done it just exactly like you wanted it done."

With the coming of spring our minds were on the new house again. All winter we had time to live with the plans in a dreamy way, trying them out. No big changes came to my mind, but small changes did and in most cases they were simplifications.

I had to be very determined and belligerent. So I said:

"I don't want another house just crammed down my throat. If I can't have a few things to say about how this one is built, I don't see any reason to go to all the trouble of building it, because I might as well just keep on living in one of the ones we already have."

I felt a twinge of disloyalty to the houses we had lived in and loved, and I felt I was running a great risk in saying such a thing. But there it was, and I was sticking to my guns.

For months there was an undercurrent of strain. Both of us tried to straighten things out openly. Sometimes we managed to do it. Most of the time our discussions would start with Sted saying, "I'm just going to do it my way."

I was afraid, but piled on more abuse. I had dreams at night—once that the moon was falling out of the sky at a crazy angle. I said, "Sted, the world is coming to an end!" And I threw my arms around him to make up for all the hurt I had caused him.

He put his arms around me and said, "No, the world isn't coming to an end. Just keep calm."

The war was still on. Building material was conscripted for Los Alamos and it was almost impossible to get anything. Besides doing the cooking, it was my job to get the building material, as I had known it would be. I had friends everywhere in the lumber business doing their level best to save me what we needed.

If I came home with a nail a quarter of an inch longer or shorter than Sted wanted, he took his irritation out on me. I knew it was because of the undercurrent caused by what I'd said, so I gritted my teeth or snapped back at him.

It was hard on the boys. Once, during a hot argument, they went outside, and in a little while Wilfred came back in. I was sitting in Sted's lap with my head on his shoulder and my arms around his neck. I smiled at Wilfred.

He said, "For gosh sakes, make up your minds. One minute you fight and the next you're kissing. Tom's out in the shop. I'll go tell him it's calm. Now don't start it again!"

But the undercurrent was still strong. I tried to tell Sted he was good for me and that I loved him.

"Let's forget it," he said.

The summer storms came and cleared away. My doctor told me to take it easy or I would have a nervous breakdown. He said, "That's what you get for marrying a genius."

Sted said, "What have you got that would give you a nervous breakdown? I'm the one who should have a nervous breakdown."

Friends would often drop down around four o'clock to swim and see how the house was coming. As luck would have it, they nearly always came when they shouldn't have. We would fix them drinks (I always had orange juice for myself) and sit to chat, but Sted's eyes would be watching me. I would look him straight in the eye.

One would have thought I was the guest, the way he watched me and addressed all his statements to me. He was holding my eyes so that I wouldn't look too much on one of our gentlemen guests. He thought I liked this friend. And I did.

This certain friend seemed to be a reverberation; another representation of a type I had always found easy to like. He was the little boy in school who fought with me and put my hair in his inkwell, the uncle who played the violin, and the boy at the wishing well. He gave me a lift and it seemed that he was in need of a lift, too. There was just a feeling of quiet approval between us.

One morning I made some comment on how nicely the house was shaping up, and Sted said, "Oh, you like it, do you? It isn't just another house crammed down your throat? I ought to give you a swift kick in the pants."

There it was, out in the full sunlight. The pants or the jeans I would never wear again, no matter what I was doing. I must wear a skirt and be a woman to signify a receptivity to his ideas, instead of competing with the expressive nature that is fundamentally male in quality. If he had said that to me a month earlier, it might have been the end of our world together, but now it came as a relief.

One dark night we heard a whirr, whirr, whirr, whirr, and Sted said, "Don't strike a light. I think there's a military convoy passing on the highway."

We looked and could just make out the dark shapes passing toward Santa Fe without headlights.

"They're from Los Alamos. Some secret event is about to take place."

That was the convoy of atomic bomb parts taken for assemblage at Alamagordo. This was 1946.

World War II stopped abruptly with the dropping of the bomb at Hiroshima. It brought an implication of radical change for the average person, who had no mental preparation for such a thing. No one could have been more surprised than Sted at the atomic bomb, even though he had worked on part details that indicated war arms and explosives of some kind. Later he was given a citation from the President of the United States for his participation in the development of the bomb.

Our own personal problems seemed to be a part of the whole world problem. Understanding comes mainly through experience. If circumstances don't furnish the experience people want, they may create their own experience. I could feel Sted thinking of the companion he might have had, and I was wondering what life might have been like if I'd married someone else. Someone who thought the same kind of thoughts. We wouldn't have much money, but we'd like the same kind of music and books; devoted to each other.

I could float around on such a dream cloud, but soon the cloud would tip with too much sameness. I found myself in tears, falling back on Sted. When I came back to earth I found myself in the kitchen preparing a meal—with a tight compressed feeling of loneliness in my chest sapping the energy out of my whole body...loneliness for Sted, because we had each been thinking of someone else. It seemed awfully silly to be lonely for a husband who was just in the next room. Sometimes, I would go in to him and give him a kiss between the eyebrows.

He'd say, "Hello, Sweetie, how've you been?"

"Lonesome for you."

How had I gotten into such a whirlpool? I wanted a place at his side, instead of lagging behind him like a squaw. With experience I had developed in a way that could be a balance to his practical nature, if he would only appreciate the fact, but he wouldn't. He would say, "Tell me..." I would start and he would say, "Oh, shut up."

So I became confused if I started to express an opinion to him, or to anyone, in his presence. For a while, I wondered if headaches had affected my mind, because so often I lost a thread of thought in the middle of a sentence.

Then, after talking to Carrel one day, I realized that the confusion only came when Sted was around. He knocked the thoughts right out of my head so strongly in opposition to whatever I might have to say.

Now, I could laugh at the situation. It seemed really funny, that one person could do such a thing to another. "It is no wonder he thinks I am inarticulate."

Carrel said, "I've never had any trouble following what you have to say. I've always found you exceptionally interesting."

Good old friends. So often the tension of a married couple can be relieved by a wider circle.

One Sunday, I went out in the yard to call Sted to lunch. I called and he said, "Yo-ho" in answer.

Then I saw him with his big garden snips in his hands, quietly snipping the last piece of our beautiful Virginia Creeper vine that grew thirty feet up into a cottonwood tree. He had snipped it loose at the base of the tree "to clean up around the tree," he said.

I froze in my tracks. Many times I had asked him to look at the vine when it was in full color, but he never had time to look. It wasn't in color now because it was wintertime, and he only saw it as so much trash.

When I could move, I turned around and fled back into the house and into my room. That beautiful vine! I was fighting mad. My head was splitting. Sted and the boys ate their lunch by themselves. "Mama has a headache," Sted told the boys.

Wilfred came into the room in a few minutes to tell me that friends were coming down the road. I didn't dare show myself in such a mood. This friend was he who wouldn't have cut the vine!

"Tsk, tsk," I heard my mother say in a still small voice. "This is what I was always afraid would happen someday. It's your heart that's splitting, not your head."

I was too tired to tsk tsk back at her, or to argue. The cutting of the vine made me so confused I didn't know if I wanted to fight or not. Was Nature trying to split us up, or was she stirring us up in a melting pot? Was she through with us as a combination? "No, I won't have it that way."

There were a staggering number of broken alliances in those days, as there had been following World War I, and to me, who had lived so long with a man who always kept things in good repair, it seemed a sheer waste of good material.

Everyone could tell each other what was wrong, but one doesn't mend a fence by picking at the weak spot expecting it to be ashamed of itself and mend its own weakness. One goes to get a good piece of wire to put in the weak spot. Good piece, good traits: combined good points should mend our fences.

Maybe Sted would see my good points if he noticed I was aware of his. I thought of how he was always striving for perfection in everything, to give his family the very best possible; how happy we always were, working together. It seemed that nothing was ever wrong with any part of it. All through everything was the feeling of oneness. I raised my eyes to the mountains and I thought about this.

One night when I went to the bedroom, I looked down at Sted and he seemed to be asleep. I stood for a while expecting him to open his eyes or snore a little. When he did neither, I went on to my bed.

In the morning I said, "Were you asleep last night when I went to bed?"

"Did it look like I was playing possum?"

I fell over on the bed and laughed, and told him I was glad he could play possum, confident that there was no need for him to worry. Our friend that he was worried about was strictly forbidden fruit by my own intention. Thoughts leave us and go out to look over green pastures, but in the end they must return to where they belong.

CHAPTER 16

About this time I had another dream about my brother Wayne. He hadn't written to me but once in all the years I had lived in the West. And that letter came a few months after we'd moved, at a period when we were having a very hard time.

His letter had been enthusiastic because he wanted to move out here and have a dude ranch. I had left the answering of the letter to my practical husband, because I had a weakness for any idea of a pioneer type and knew only too well that I thought of things the way I wanted to think of them, not as they might work. Sted answered Wayne's letter, and we heard no more from him. For seven years, I thought he was deliberately not answering my subsequent letters.

When I went down to Beaumont, Texas, for my parents' fiftieth wedding anniversary, I saw him every evening and from the first moment I knew we were still friends.

He still loved music and books and we talked for hours each night. We looked at the moon through the porch screen and I saw a cross. He saw it too. A cross stood for a cause. I knew that all ideas have to be practical, or they are of no use. It was plain to me that Wayne was in no way a practical person. My heart ached as I listened to him play the mouth harp or strum his banjo.

I thought about the cross made by the moonlight on the screenwire—power and constructive creation, the mating sign of the ancients, the sign of planting. I thought of the twelfth verse in first Genesis: "And the earth brought forth grass, and herb yielding seed after his kind, and the tree yielding fruit, whose seed is in itself, after his kind: and God saw that it was good," and I knew that Wayne was good even though not at all practical. That visit haunted me for a long time after I had returned home.

Because of this reunion of sorts, the message in the latest dream made sense. In it, he was back in Houston among his old friends. My mother and my dad were there and he was happy to be back. I was there, too, in his sweetheart's old home. The house was more elegant than ever.

We were in the living room alone, and I noticed the andirons in the fireplace were exactly like some we had. As I was looking at them, they turned from simple, slightly tarnished ones to very ornate, with rosebuds which sparkled like dew in a dazzling sunlight.

I wrote to my brother and told him about the dream. But the return letter came to me from someone else, saying that my dream was amazing because my brother was in the act of selling his house so that he could move back to Houston and was very pleased and encouraged by my letter. I wrote several more letters and conspired with him to help him on this new start.

Then a letter came that he had passed away.

I thought of the andirons' dazzling brightness: "out of this world," I had written. I couldn't believe it, and grieved and fought for an answer to many things. It was impossible for me to go to his funeral. I wasn't well at this time and was mentally exhausted.

All his old friends would be there—his boyhood friends, like in the dream! Night after night I expected to have another, or some explanation to quiet my feelings.

I felt cursed for a lack of understanding. At this point, Sted told Carrel that the trouble with me was that I was more woman than most women. I did feel like the curse of all women had fallen on me, driving me to face death. My mother used to remind me that "the wages of sin is death."

We had always waged a silent war on the subject of marriage, and now I remembered that I'd made a vow to myself to enjoy marriage even if I had to be a sinful woman and have a sinful man. Was "sin" itself trying to take its toll of me? If so, let it come. The death of man will never kill the spirit of love. And in that spirit will someday be found two factors of Mind, married!

I felt delirious. I was striving so hard to understand life and death and Mind and mind.

Sixteen days after my brother's death, I was in the hospital waiting for a radium implant. It was all wrong, but what could I do? I promised myself that I would search until I found a clear understanding of a universal measure.

The doctor came in and picked up my hand and said, "Your hands are warm. You're not nervous, are you?"

"No, I'm in your hands. Take care of me; I've made myself a promise I have to keep."

"Good, you'll snap right out of this."

(Bedside manner cures more ills than pills, I think.)

Old one-eyed Joaquin came to the hospital to see me. I was pleased and touched. I reached out and found the fifty-cent piece in my little painted box. It was coined in the year of my birth. Joaquin had given it to me for good luck.

"Mr. Stedman feel awful bad here," Joaquin said, as he put his hand over his heart. "The goman be the heart of the house, and when she not be there, the house be not the same."

In the quiet loneliness of that hospital room, I had to find an answer.

Was my brother's life ended, locked forever in the grave? Or had he found better conditions, as the dream indicated, and freedom? A science teacher a long time ago had told me that nothing was ever lost, that things changed forms; solids into gases, gases into liquids. Isn't there something of our life or mind, a part of a universal natural element that changes but doesn't go out of existence, and is more important than the small amount of dust our bodies leave?

"I have to know. Please tell me," I asked of that universal knowledge which I believe to be available to one with an open mind.

I closed my eyes and searched in the darkness for a vision, an answer in image, like I do when I want to see a painting that I want to paint. I held my question in mind so that no stray thoughts would interfere. Then I began to see a strong dark head and hands held before the chest of a figure.

The hands were holding a jewel box between the upright fingers. The whole thing looked like a sculptor's creation of stone and clay, strong and beautiful. The head slowly reclined with eyes closed as though asleep and the hands were like jagged upright stone and earth.

"Mother Earth," of course. Now the hands held the lid of the box open and the box was buried in her solar plexus. I looked deep into the box and saw bluewhite bones through brilliant gaseous light, and then the gases escaped and drifted upwards, white, blue-white and yellow. They twirled like a cornucopia and revealed a figure as they drifted upwards.

The posture, the droop of the shoulders, and the tilt of the head, everything about it was my brother. I held this picture until the gasses curled around the figure and obscured it from my sight. Then, to the right further off appeared a colonial staircase and balustrade and a girl in a Martha Washington costume was slowly descending.

It was his deceased sweetheart wife, Gertrude. The costume was one she wore to one of the community plays. I had painted a portrait of her in that costume. There was a young man obviously her lover, descending the staircase with her.

It was my brother but time had been set back. His arm was through hers and his other hand covered her hand which rested on their linked arms and they were smiling at each other. While my mind searched the rest of the picture, warm shadows outlined the face and hands of Mother Earth but softly as though a cloud was dulling down this part, and when I looked beyond in a cool full flood of moonlight there was a garden and the lovers were seated on a white ornamental wrought-iron bench.

This must be a trick of my mind and the subconscious result of having read recently that all things return to be a part of nature's memory. I must try again for the correct answer. The boundaries of my body began to fall away and I seemed to float for a long while through space and darkness. Then there seemed to be deep fathomless water below me and I was suspended in space as a hummingbird.

I looked up and saw a light and a huge hand holding the light and then the whole figure became visible. It was the Statue of Liberty, the symbol of freedom. I held the image for what seemed a long while and can see both of these pictures plainly now or anytime.

Slowly, I became conscious of my body again and I knew that I had the answer. Never again would I doubt that the real part of us was a forever part, and a new sense of freedom and joy overcame my sorrow.

When I returned home, I rested and continued my reading and

thinking. Even during sleep my mind was searching. When the village church bell rang, I wished that I could jump into the kitchen and rattle the pots and pans around, get a good Sunday morning breakfast ready, hustle my family up and into their Sunday best and off to church. My family would think I was mad.

Sted said that people always look for God when they're in trouble. They want someone to lean on, and to forgive their sins and to tell them what to think. So what? I wasn't proud. I felt lost and alone. Only by finding a true conformation concerning the nature of God could I feel a part of anything again. The church at least pretended to have an understanding.

At lunch one day, Sted asked me what was wrong. "You seem to be sick all the time. Is it mental?"

My eyes filled with tears and I left the table. If I blurted out all the things on my mind, I would find myself carted off to the nut house. He listened to murder mysteries and threats of a third world war. Talk of God and love and harmony - it just wouldn't do. Yet it was the tenderness in his voice that made my eyes fill with tears, and some of the loneliness was gone. We were somehow in touch again.

Carrel and Bill came in, and another pair of old friends. Sted was playing the accordion. Bill took a dime out of his pocket and flipped it at Sted's feet. He continued to play and the house filled with laughter and song. Tom played a few tunes. This was a wonderful thing—to have a family, neighbors and friends, songs and music. I went into the kitchen to get cokes and beer. The gnawing in my insides was gone for the moment.

I listened calmly as the telegram announcing my mother's death was read to me over the phone. Sted patted my hand and said, "I'm sorry."

"Breakfast is ready. Let's eat before the eggs get cold."

"You ought to go, kid."

"Go? I hadn't thought of going. There isn't anything I can do."

"You'll never feel right about it if you don't go," he told me.

"You're right. I should go and help my father through this."

I'd never been on a plane before. Though my brother Ralph was killed in a plane crash, he had believed in planes.

"I'll call and see about your reservation while you start packing."

For some reason I had gotten up in the night and bathed and washed my hair.

On the way to the plane I said, "Sted, I want you to know that I don't feel badly about this thing. For the past year I've been expecting it."

"It's been longer than that. Four years ago she almost passed away. When people get old they can't last forever."

As we sat out in the sun waiting for the plane to arrive, I said, "I've been living over my whole childhood and all of my past these last few months. When I come back, we'll live for the future."

He was quiet and didn't look at me. He waved and held his hand aloft until the plane took off and I could see him no more.

"Doggone him," I cried within. "He's the dearest person on earth to me. I tell him and tell him, but it goes in one ear and out the other without leaving a dent in his brain."

Next to him and the boys was my mother, but I found no need to cry for her now, because I'd done all my crying the past few months. Several times in the past years I had written to her, telling her how much she always meant to me. She was independent and aggressive, which sometimes overshadowed us all, but underneath I was just as independent. So now I could think of it as an asset, an active strength. It got things done.

After all the years of tsk tsking about our Christian Science neighbors, Mother had a Christian Science funeral. She'd been studying it for two years, though she had never mentioned it to me. And I suspect her type of service was someone else's idea.

I was startled by these lines as read in the service: "Spirit is God, and man is His image and likeness. Therefore man is not material; he is spiritual." This was from the Christian Science textbook, "Science and Health With Key To The Scriptures" by Mary Baker Eddy.

I was torn between a feeling of guilt for not knowing this truth as stated, and a feeling that I remembered a truth that is more encompassing: that all material is spiritual material, sometimes visible, sometimes invisible, man included.

When I was alone in the yard at my father's, my mind seemed to float into a brown void and look back on me lying in a hammock until someone spoke my name.

I spent two weeks out on the farm with my father. We talked about Mother. We both felt she had been a very unusual person, closer to other forms of life than most of us. He told me how all the cows and horses stayed near the house and barn lot the night she died instead of going out to pasture. They bawled and bawled. Even the atoms in the wood of the house must have stirred. She had loved that house, too. All one had to do was look around.

My younger brother Harrell, whom I had not seen for fourteen years arrived. I had thought he was on a boat off Japan, but he happened to be in New York for a few days and flew down. He pushed me in a great swing hanging from a large oak tree and we walked down a dusty road lined with coffee bean trees. We sat on a bridge; the stale brown water with the turtles hanging by their noses to the surface, the weeds and flowers and our relationship exactly as they always were.

That night I went to sleep thinking of Sted. I dreamt that I was a child, barefoot, walking along a road. I came to two puddles of water with a thin strip of damp earth separating them. I dipped my big toe in one puddle and pulled it across the strip of ground to the other pool, and to my amazement the water from the first puddle followed my toe and drained into the second pool, leaving the first one empty. It was as plain as day what this dream meant: Sted was the pool I had drained and, seeing it, I felt his emptiness. I must get home.

Houston friends had heard from Sted about how much I had helped him in planning and building our houses; they asked my advice about their own homes. One friend, an architect, said Sted had told him I was not only a good draftsman and designer, but the best foreman he ever had. This only confused me further. What should I believe?

My mother appeared beside me on the train. I wasn't thinking about her. Or dreaming. She seemed to come of herself as she used to do when I was a little child, to see if I were all right. I pretended to be asleep.

That vision of the brown void I experienced in the hammock held my attention. It had been dark, then filled with light. There was sound. It seemed to have a great significance that I couldn't get hold of. Maybe I was just plain nuts and a fear gripped me tight again, as though I were guilty of some terrible crime.

There was no one, that I knew of, thinking as I was thinking at that time.

Chapter 17

At home, I complained about the radio. Always talk of distrust, deceit, murder and a third war.

Sted said, "It's an escape for me. I'll listen to what I like and you read what you like."

I said, "But that puts you at one extreme and me at the other. Can't we find some middle ground?"

"By your attitude lately it seems to me you've been deliberately trying to sabotage all our plans, and I'll never be able to trust you again."

He went out the door saying, "You've disappointed me and I've disappointed you."

"You haven't disappointed me," I cut in.

"You always do things in such a sketchy way, skipping over details."

"Those are unimportant things," I said. He went off and I started singing—of all things!

He didn't have any reason to distrust me. He only thought he might, if he knew all the details he thought I could have provided.

But there were no details to provide. He'd been worrying while I was gone about how much our friend might mean to me and, as luck would have it, our friend happened by and was talking to me just as Sted drove up to pick me up on my return home. All our friend had said to me was, "Are you feeling better now?" referring to my mother's death. He and Sted were good friends; I was the culprit without having done anything but fight to keep my senses.

On top of all this we started to build another house. It was the summer of 1950. Our twenty-one year old son Tom was the head engineer. Tom would be entering his fourth year of college in engineering in the fall. Wilfred, sixteen, entering his first year of college the same fall, as a pre-med student, worked with him and a small crew on the new house.

Before we started the house, Sted had taken me for a walk on the new place. He asked me, "Where would you like a new house, Mrs. Stedman?"

"Up at the other place, in the community. I want to keep our own house with plenty of elbow room."

He did what I wanted, but there was a fight about this, because he wanted to build it for sale and I wanted to keep it to rent. We kept it.

I heard him tell the boys, "Your mother is an intellectual. Don't ever think she doesn't know what she's doing."

I didn't know what being an intellectual had to do with keeping the house. It was either a rare compliment or sarcasm. I wasn't sure how he meant it. But it didn't sound like sarcasm.

One day there was a lot of shopping for me to do. It was all I could do to keep from crying all over town, crying for Sted because I wanted so much to have everything all right between us. It was late when I got home and he met me with a smile and kiss, and then by the fire later he asked me if I still loved him.

"Yes I do." And I could have wept with joy.

"I love you, too. It was awfully quiet and lonesome around here today while you were gone. I thought maybe you'd never come back. That's why I get so mad at you when you go off; I'm afraid you won't come back, get a nice supper and sit with me by the fire."

"You said those exact words the evening we were married, after I'd been away from you for a few hours to buy my wedding dress. Why do you think that I wouldn't come home?"

"Because when you're gone I think about how mean I've been."

"I'm glad you were. I've learned a lot that I never would have otherwise. You've learned something, too."

"I guess we're doomed to each other."

I remembered the wishing well, the clear feeling that I was destined to marry a man who would push me under deep water that would teach me enriching things.

The two of us were alone in the house. Our house, a mixture of ideas and efforts born with such pain, now so peaceful and beautiful this night. We sat in front of the fire and were at home with each other, in a "...house not made with hands..." (II Corinthians 5:1)

The next morning at breakfast, he put his hand over mine and said to me, "We are soul mates, you and I. Not even death can part our hands."

I had a gut feeling that I was going to be alone sooner or later...with a space of time to arrive at the understanding of what he just said.

Sted had arthritis in his right hip joint, which was completely destroying the joint and making it almost impossible for him to walk. There was nothing doctors could do about it. The mere thought that he would soon be reduced to a wheelchair was killing him.

"You'll never see arthritis given as a cause of death," he told me. And after a chair tipped backwards, throwing him on the floor, his shoulder became painful. I took him to the hospital one Sunday morning to have it X-rayed. He said, "If they find arthritis in my shoulder, I'm not going to be able to take it, kid."

"The X-ray shows you have some arthritis here..."

Sted simply nodded his head in agreement. We went home. I found him sitting down on a little stool, crying. It was the only time in my life I saw him cry. I knelt beside him and wept on his knees.

I had a dream that if he would go to church he would be healed. He got in the car with me and I took him to St. Francis Cathedral in downtown Santa Fe. I stopped right at the entrance but he just sat there. I pulled away.

"Myrtle, I'd give anything to have your faith. I know that is part of my problem but you can't teach an old dog new tricks. I know when you're helping me. I have times of total relief from pain when I see you in meditation, or whatever it is you're doing."

I saw death in his face. It became impossible for me to do anything for him. He walked to the car himself to go to the hospital.

"I hate to take you to the hospital."

"Why?"

"Because they'll just dope you up until you won't know anything."

But my real reason was that I instinctively knew he wouldn't be walking back into his own house again.

He was in hospital about four days. In that time he developed one symptom after another. Dr. Angle tried frantically to do something for him. I came into his room and he said, "Goodbye."

"Tell me hello, not goodbye." But I knew from the look of finality in his eyes that it was "goodbye" by his own creative design.

The hospital priest came and wanted to give him the last rites. I shook my head—then ran down the hall after him to come back. It was ironic that I should do this when Sted wasn't in the position to say "no."

I wasn't sure whether he heard anything the priest said—and I know that I didn't. But there was one thing I mightily had to say to Sted.

I leaned over him and shouted, though it was actually only a whisper, "Sted, I want you to know that I've never been unfaithful to you. I've never loved anyone but you."

He looked at me and I knew he heard and believed.

And then he was gone.

Chapter 18

A dark abyss opened before me and I retreated with fear and trembling. Then I saw a light reach out and return to its beginning. And the abyss rose and fell with this turning to and return and was enlightened by the activity. The light was shadowed and there was form.

And the whole universe acknowledged the consummation and rejoiced.

And I heard this saying: Four stages lead to wisdom and understanding.

And I saw that the oneness of mind and of all of its forms is based on a love common to all.

Imagine, if you can, an infinite death-like before-time rest—virgin mind in semi-conscious repose. Close your eyes and all is darkness as far as you can see. Watch, for there is a quickening and a flickering of light to be observed. Then rest again while you contemplate what you have seen. But look, for the darkness quickens again and the light is at hand.

She stirs with another quickening and sighs, and quickens again and again in a chain until it becomes a necessity for the light to possess her and she him.

And where she draws him she follows; so that there is a breathing increasing until it mounts to an agonized stillness. Then there is a blinding flash and an explosive declaration in the giving and the taking. After the recession and when there is again a period of rest, and change can be observed, there is light and darkness, divided, yet one. And the darkness is pregnant with form.

Except for the darkness of the mind longing for the light of the mind, there would be no beings visible in form, nor any tangible ideas separated from the intangible. All space is spaced and placed with forms of light and darkness. All forms are sensitive—and all are consciously motivated so that there is a prevailing spirit—a will and a willingness to be and to "Let there be" multitudinous forms of the mind.

Light is the brilliance of the mind—darkness gives it depth and form.

———

It's so ridiculous, I thought as I sat flanked by my two sons at my husband's funeral service, that we know so little about such important things.

One morning, just the week before, Sted had said, "I dreamt I saw you and the boys in black, and the whole house was filled with artists, writers and people we know. But nobody paid any attention to me when I tried to talk to them. I went from one to the other; finally I got so mad I tried to get them all out of the house."

I looked around this new, appropriately sparsely furnished house that we had just built and in which we had lived during his last few weeks. There were Gus Baumann and Jane, Theodore Van Soelen and Virginia, Raymond Jonson and Vera, Fremont Ellis and Randall Davey, Reginald Fisher (director of the New Mexico Museum of Fine Arts) and his wife Grace, painter Odon Hullenkremer, author Oliver LaFarge and Consuelo, George Fitzpatrick and Opal, Alan Vedder and his wife, residents of our Old Ranch House, and many more.

There were relatives, some we hadn't seen for years. There was even the lady from down the road who ran the Post Office and liquor store. She'd never had a civil word for any of us but she brought a pie.

All I could think of was Sted, angry, trying to get us all out of his house.

I must have looked strange. I felt desperate. I remember the boys tugging at my arms, trying to get me to listen to the calm assurance given by artist Stanley Breneiser, who looked for all the world like the minister Dr. Ryan of Houston who married us. He took great care in the selections he read for the occasion—things, he later told me, that he thought particularly appropriate for the creative group of people he knew would be there.

I wanted nothing to do with the whole thing. I felt Sted's presence and aliveness—not his death.

The boys were manly and quiet. I felt their nearness and their strength. The casket was in front of the Indian corner fireplace with flowers banked on its several ledges. Odon Hullenkremer gave Sted's chest a rap with the back of his knuckles as he passed by. I had deliberately not appointed pallbearers, knowing that those who wanted would give a hand.

It was past mid-September. I had been conscious of the golden light flooding the rooms. Outside, it fell in shafts through the apple tree leaves. The chamisa along the highway was in full bloom, and the purple asters.

The night Sted died, friends had gathered. Our very close friend took me in his arms and said, "Now that he's gone, you will let me come and see you, won't you?"

"No. You have your wife."

"And how I love that little girl. But I can love you both."

"No." And I wouldn't let him write an eulogy for Sted, even though it would have meant a lot to all of us, especially Sted.

The next morning I got a phone call. The person at the other end of the phone said, "Look, you're going to need someone to look after you. I'm an able-bodied man and I'd like to marry you." I said, "Don't you ever call me again."

It was close to Christmas. I received a card from a sculptor friend. He wrote: "I hope you have the best Christmas of your life." What was I supposed to think of that? A few days later an architect called and wanted me to have dinner with him. I said, "No thanks, I can't."

He said, "Why not? I thought we'd have a lot in common."

Later, one Sunday morning, I was walking along my place on the highway. I had a shovel and was going to do some irrigating. A car pulled up and, right in the middle of the highway, I got another marriage proposal.

Old one-eyed Joaquin said to me one day as we were mending a fence, "You think too much." And he put his arm around me. I jumped away and said, "Don't touch me!" He said, "Don't be afraid of me. I love you like I love my mother."

What was I thinking about?

I was thinking about Sted saying, "You make people think you're in love with them." I was thinking about how he dragged me into bed one evening when we were dressing to go to a party.

I asked, "Why now?" He said, "To cool you down before we go out."

I was thinking about him saying another day, "If I could think of some worthy cause, I'd give this ranch away." I said, "You would do that to us? Why?" He answered, "There are no separate property rights for women. I just hate to think of someone else marrying you and getting all I've worked for. You like being married so much you'd be married again before the year was up."

I was thinking about Tom's sudden marriage—that he didn't let me in on until he'd done it—just a month after Sted's death. I was thinking of him asking: "Mom, are you going to give Marion and me the Cotton-woods?" And my answer: "No, I am not."

"You should move into one of the smaller houses on the other ranch. It would be a waste for you to occupy the Cottonwoods by yourself."

God, I thought, didn't your mother teach you any manners?

I was thinking about Sted's promise to see Wilfred through college, medical school and internship. I was thinking about "Of One Mind" I had written:

"The Mind's whole nature is to be One."

My writings were like the finalization of an architectural plan. All the ideas, on paper, showed me the oneness of an embrace unbroken by death—an embrace based on the very composition of the Mind. How much substance does that Creative Mind put into a single expression of itself?

Should I open my eyes to the Man of the Mind as all men, or keep them on the one man who worked to gain the title of the land we owned, who took himself seriously as an individual—an architect and artist?

Sted had long ceased to believe in the God of his childhood. He had claimed to be an agnostic. Yet he had said: "We will be together always." He had promised that if it were at all possible to communicate with me after he was gone, he would.

It remained for me to see how strong his sense of immortality was. What was immortality if it didn't include "here and now," or didn't display the expressive and the receptive nature of the Mind as one inseparable whole? Could I carry on expressing the male qualities as well as the female qualities as long as I retained a sense of these as figures of speech?

In our twenty-three years of living and working together, I was not always listening to Sted; I found in the end it was good sometimes to make him listen to me. But in the main, he was more expressive than receptive, yet receptive, too. His life was predominantly a continuous projection of information about art and architecture. He gave me all he knew and thought.

All this was not gone. I had it, and more. I was not always graciously receptive, being also of an expressive nature.

The day Sted's body was being cremated, a host of angels came and sang to me, filling a portion of the sky with their bright presence. I drew in the words of their singing and felt the impact of eternal truths. I was lying in the back seat of the car in the park at the Albuquerque Zoo; my whole family strolled among the animals.

A few nights afterwards, I was sitting alone with my big dog stretched out at my feet. The dog lifted its head and moved its tail as though to wag it. He turned his head to look at an apparition we both sensed was standing in a familiar doorway.

I was pleased and happy—though realizing there was nothing further we could do about it. I just mentally told him, "tough luck." Christ's return is the only one given credence in our Western culture.

I don't know what I would have done had he cooked up some fish and bidden me to breakfast, as Jesus Christ did after He had risen from the dead. The dog drooped his head and sighed.

At other times, both asleep and awake, there was a sense of Sted's presence which left me transfigured. I went about glowing. Friends asked one another and even asked me: "Are you getting married again?"

No. I still wore his ring and was still Mrs. Stedman. I felt that we had only skimmed the surface of marriage, and that he and I had more to do. I had the recurring dream that we were just separated. In my dream I tried to convince him that I missed him and there was a great yearning to have him back, but he held himself aloof.

In that very aloofness there was a feeling that he wasn't through with me.

Shortly before Sted's death, we had rented out the Cottonwoods and temporarily lived in the house we were building. We were to finish it, sell it, then winter in Old Mexico. Both boys were in college. Marian Hardie, the girl Tom had since married, was also at the University of New Mexico at that time. Tom and Marion were married by a Justice of the Peace on a day that they both had exams. To satisfy Marion's religious feeling and to announce their wedding publicly, they married again in January at the Presbyterian Church in Santa Fe. We had a small reception at this unfinished house.

Then I was left alone there, except for my old shepherd-collie dog. After the cremation, Tom had been very solicitous to me and had told me that, since he was the elder son, he felt he should look after me from now on. I'd said, "You have your own life to live, I'll be all right"—which reminded me of another thing Sted had said: "You'll be a rich woman when I die." And my answer to that had been: "I'm far richer having you than I'll ever be without you."

But I knew I would never be without him. We had packed so much into our twenty-three years together that I knew it would last me a lifetime and beyond.

My widowed father came and subsequently lived with me for eight years, with intermittent stays with my sister in Houston. I took the unfinished house off the market, finished it, and settled up all the business of paying the materials and labor bills.

I did a few illustrations for New Mexico Magazine, filling Sted's place until they could get a new art editor and illustrator. I finished up work that we had started for the New Mexico Tourist Bureau. I did some designing to be cast in Nambe Ware, and re-typed and re-edited my book, "Of One Mind," and finished the drawings for it.

In the fall we had a bumper crop of apples. My father helped me sell them, though he was so blind he could only feel the money to make small change. When he had first come to me, he told me I would have to lift the coffee cup for him. But I'd said, "Daddy, you've been a builder all your life. You know distance, and how to use your hands." He made it from then on.

My father was about five feet eight. He was lean and sinewy from all his years as a builder. His stomach was concave, hard and muscular; his arms strong, brown and hairy with a good pair of hands. His head was bald and shiny, except for a fringe of dark graying hair. His cheekbones were high on his tanned face, his eyes brown and pleasant. He was a handsome figure in gray flannel and plaid.

He was always "Dad Kelly" at home and always "Dad Kelly" here with all of my friends. The women always made a fuss over him. He was soft-spoken and quiet most of the time, but when he did speak it was often sparked with quirks of humor. He spent a lot of time in the big chair in front of the fire.

He would always want to know, "What are you going to do today, Myrtle?" It bothered him that he couldn't help me on the houses, but he answered the phone and was a presence on the place when I was out.

A painting I did of him in 1933 hangs on my studio wall. It is a strong painting, built on the principle of dynamic symmetry. You can see it from the far end of the house. He is sitting with his legs wrapped around his own handmade device which clamps a saw. He always filed his own saws. There are angular shapes of color around him to evoke the god-awful sound of the filing, a frame house under construction in the background, and him placidly sucking a dead pipe while filing.

This painting and others of mine afforded a lot of material for a Rice Institute psychology professor at the time they hung in a show at the Houston Fine Arts Museum in 1933. A friend of mine was in the class and told me, "Myrtle, you should have been there. You would have liked the way he talked about your paintings."

When I rented out the finished new house and we moved back to the Cottonwoods, my father carried feed to the horses, shook my rugs, washed my dishes, went up to the highway to collect our daily mail, and kept the fire going in the fireplace by day.

By night, he covered the logs with ashes and in the morning he pulled away the ash and put in another log. An adobe house can be cool enough for a fire in the fireplace even in the summer.

On warm days he would sit in the patio at the back of the house and listen to the river. The Indians were still using horses and wagons in the 1950s and travelled along the river way. Sometimes, when they would see my father sitting in the patio, they would tie their horses to a cottonwood tree and climb up the bank to my patio.

I could see the silver thread of the river from my kitchen window, so when I would see them stop I would make coffee and cut cake or get out cookies so they could sit, sip, nibble and talk.

They would talk about the weather, present and how it used to be, and they would talk about their crops or a broken wagon tongue. Sometimes they would invite us to a dance and say, "Come to my house." This meant that when there was a pause in the dance we could disappear into one of their houses with them. The room would be full of Indians and a few privileged Anglo friends, talking and eating. A big table was always set with lots of food—green chili and meat, turkey, deer, pinto beans, corn on the cob, bread pudding and bread cooked outside in the round adobe ovens. The drums would take me quietly out to experience with the Indians the deep mystery between man and the great spirit in all nature. This would invariably bring rain out of a cloudless sky.

The old dog, Lucky, was my father's constant companion. Dad said, "When you're away, though, he must lie out in the yard waiting for your return, because I can't get him to stay with me." One of my boys told me that Sted had told him in a dream: "Your mother is looking after two old men...the old dog and her father."

I wasn't sure who was looking after whom.

Robins had always come to the ranch in flocks in the spring, dotting whole fields. Some stayed on after nesting, all summer and into the fall. Sted had loved to sit at his end of the long table and look out at the robins in the big field. He liked the dignified way they went about feeding themselves on worms—unhurried and with a confident strike at the right moment, at the right place.

With as much nonchalance as an Englishman in spats using his cane to flick up some imagined object, they would pick out a worm and eat it like a delicacy from a well-set table laid with fine linen and silver candelabra.

A robin's front was like a prosperous Englishman's bay window, breasted in a russet vest. All that was lacking was a heavy gold chain spanning the expanse from clip to watch in pocket. The robins didn't walk—they strutted.

Sted had said, "They act like they own the place."

"I can see you as a robin."

"When I live again, I'd like to be one."

That winter, a robin stayed through a blizzard, after the worms were frozen stiff. Robins don't eat seed.

"The silly thing," I thought, "why doesn't it go away?" It flew into the window Sted used to watch from. The window was fixed—I couldn't open it. I tried the others.

I told it, "If you are Sted you should know where the door is." I tried to coax it; it stayed around three days and nearly drove me mad. At last it flew so hard against the studio window that it knocked itself out, dead.

I let it lie all winter. In the spring, after the ground had thawed, I took a shovel and buried it around the corner at the end of the studio.

One day followed another as one foot follows another in walking. On one such ordinary day, I was walking from my car to the front door. My father was on a visit to Houston so I was alone. The winter had been long. I heard a distinct rustling in the dried grass at the end of the studio.

That dried-up robin came up out of his shallow grave, shook the loose dirt from his feathers, walked around the corner of the studio in and onto the flagstone on the portal, looked for a moment at the place beneath the studio window where he had lain all winter, then turned and walked the full length of the portal, talking to me in chirps.

At my feet, he turned onto the flagstone walk, stopped a second to pluck at a piece of dried grass, then walked out of sight around the corner of the house.

I could see that his bill was still bent from smashing into the glass and it struck me that he was walking on a flagstone walk that I'd put down after Sted's death as though it were familiar.

I didn't follow. I let myself into the house, threw myself down on my bed, and prayed: "Please, God, release him."

And then it occurred to me that he was released, released into a realm of consciousness where thought is free to express itself in any manner in which it chooses to communicate. Who can say that the supernatural is not natural?

I had known when Sted had died because I had seen his spirit leave his body and pause above his left shoulder. It had looked down on our two sons and on me. I had lifted the covers and kissed the soles of his feet in answer—a salute to a victorious spirit.

CHAPTER 19

I had all the houses that we'd built on the ranch and there was no reason to sell them. I felt very fortunate to have them to rent, and was inspired to turn Sted's small studio at the big house into an extra bath. It had a fireplace and footprints on the hearth made by Wilfred's baby feet. A workman had lifted him through the window when the house was under construction. When I was resetting the john, Wilfred happened to come in and put his big footprints before it in the damp cement.

One night Carrel Williams called from Chicago. She and Bill had gone back there to his advertising firm. Carrel's call was about an old adobe ruin on their Tesuque property. She said, "Myrtle, Bill wants to carry out Sted's idea about doing something with that old ruin. He wants to know if you could get an architect and builder to do it for us."

I told her I could and we discussed the matter at length; then, just as I thought she was ready to hang up, she said, "What Bill would really like would be for you to design and build it. We love your houses and know how much you did to accomplish that loveliness."

I said, "I was wondering what to do with my Contractor's license."

There was a dead silence for a moment, then Carrel said, "What did I think I heard you say? That you have a Contractor's license? And so you could, if you would, do a house for us? Bill will be delighted. Myrtle, you never cease to amaze us—the things you do. Just wait until I tell Bill."

She not only told Bill, but she told their friends the Bennetts who started thinking I could do a house for them in Taos. Benny was an executive for Sweets Catalogue, the "Architect's Bible." It would be a feather in my cap to do a house for him.

I had made a fierce commitment to build an adobe house all by myself, to get full credit for it and to feel the sense of accomplishment. The first time I made that commitment, it was in a spirit of strong defiance— when I didn't get credit for designing the studio house we had made out of that old adobe ruin on our own place.

The second time was when I saw huge old carved beams and corbels in a building which, at that time, was being used for a garage, but which had originally been built as a theater. I vowed I had to build a house with such beams.

The day Carrel arrived from Chicago, she and I went looking over the old ruin. A man saw us and came over, wondering if we could use some old corbels and beams. They were the very same ones I had seen in the garage. That man was dismantling the garage to make way for the First

National Bank's new building.

Carrel thought the beams would be too big and heavy, but I knew they were my beams. When the time came, I got the well-driller with his crane to swing them up into place. They were so dirty with car exhaust that we had no idea there was color inlay in the deep carving until Carrel washed them with Oxidol soap. The colors were red, green and blue.

There were heavy, hand-made doors that came with the corbels and beams, a small narrow window, and lots of solid tongue-and-groove material. I used it all. There wasn't a new board used anywhere, except in the kitchen; we carved those and made them look old.

One old door I salvaged from the ruin. It was very plain; my carpenter had left it out. It had been in a part of the ruin where Carrel and Bill had kept a cow. When I told the carpenter, he said, "You're not going to put that old thing in this beautiful little house?"

I made him hang it, and afterwards I swung it and it squeaked on its hinges. I asked him to oil it and he said, "No, the squeak goes with an old barn door." He was the head man of my crew, and kept us in stitches with his astute and whimsical remarks all through the job. He worked for me for years: if he passed a few days without seeing me, he would call me up and say, "You dead or alive?"

When the house was all finished, Bill told me it was so beautiful it didn't need furniture. 1953.

After I finished this house, I took over the management of all four of their houses along with my own. I rented their little house to an old friend of Bill's. He had corresponded with Sted about the illustrations Sted was doing for New Mexico Magazine.

When he rented Bill's house, he told me he had come because of me. He was about Sted's height, had the same kind of art training, was a good conversationalist, and had a very interesting face and build, much like Sted's.

When Sted had said that we'd be together again, because he'd come to the conclusion we were soul-mates, I'd said: "Well, maybe I'll rent a house to you."

Could this be Sted under another name? Who knows how the Mind arranges things? I felt I had known this friend of Bill's before, and he claimed he knew where everything was in my house. When he wanted a toothpick, he knew where the box was. He taught me to cook a turkey in front of a fireplace fire. He attached it to a string and wire hanging from a hook in a viga above the fireplace.

The turkey was held in between two coat hangers fastened together to make a basket, and the string was twirled so that the turkey turned and from its own weight would twirl the other way, then back again. Once in a while we had to wind it up again, and we had to keep the fire going, but when the turkey was done it was delicious, cooked in its own inner juices without any further seasoning. Sometimes he would do a meal for me at his little house.

I became overly fond of him. My boys liked him, too; even my dog.

But one night my dog wasn't home to sleep by my bed. The next morning he bolted out of this man's house when I went to leave a note for him about looking for the dog. I was on my way to Taos for the day. He said, "Myrtle, Lucky likes me and wanted to stay with me last night." But I knew Lucky wouldn't have stayed with him unless he'd been shut in.

Suddenly I saw that this was very unlike Sted, and that I had been mesmerized by a mystical idea. He was more like me than Sted, because he wanted to know more about the mystery of life. Sted put all that kind of thing aside, yet he was more a mystery than either of us.

Chapter 20

Carrel kept asking me to think about doing a house in Taos for the Bennetts of Chicago. Three times Benny called and asked me to go up to Taos with him to look at houses. Finally, I picked Benny up at the airport and we went up, but I didn't like any of the houses. But a short way out of Taos, after we had finished looking at a place, I spotted one which was sitting by itself, four hundred feet back from the road with the mountains framing a backdrop and a view of waterfalls to the east. I told Benny, "If you could find something like that, I'd be interested." The building was a nearly abandoned Penitente morada, or meeting place.

The Penitente people were the Catholics who had been cut off from the Church because of their isolation and because of penitential practices like flagellation or hanging chosen members of their Brotherhood on a cross on Good Friday.

At one time there were many moradas in northern New Mexico. There are still a few active ones, but only one that I know of which will allow outsiders to view any Brotherhood activities. There is one on the north side of the Talpa road where, on Good Friday, you can sit on the ground or stand outside the morada and listen to the Penitentes read from their book of songs and prayers and, afterwards, view their procession along footpaths on the Talpa Ridge. They march, singing, to the straining of a flute. Andrew Dasburg, as well as other painters, had a studio on this route, and one year I was among a small group of people watching and listening.

The morada we found north of Taos had been built in 1934 and there were only about twelve families still using it. Margo Butler, our real estate agent and daughter of the late painter Bert Phillips, thought she'd heard that the Brothers wanted to abandon it and sell. She would look into the matter and let us know. A little later she informed us we could get it.

Benny said, "I guess you could use the adobes from it, Myrtle." But I said, "We can use the whole thing."

For a morada, it was large, an L-shape with a low pitched roof and a bell tower. The roof was of weathered wide boards and battens; the bell tower above the narrow front entrance had a peaked roof with a wooden cross atop. There were only five small, square, high windows. There was a pond in front of the place where the Penitentes may have had baptismal ceremonies. The pond had aspen trees ringing the side toward the road.

We couldn't know what the inside looked like until after the Brothers removed their religious artifacts. It was interesting, though, because they wanted to sell us the artifacts from one of their members houses right away—we bought the bell and took it back to our belfry. I was planning to go to Chicago for Christmas to be with Carrel and Bill and to see a Mary Cassatt show at the Chicago Fine Arts Museum when Margo called and told me she had the key to the morada.

My friend and I went up. It was a cold day. The morada was swathed in snow. When I opened the door I was so overwhelmed with its peace and quiet and beauty that I fell into his arms.

The ceiling had peeled, honey-colored aspen poles laid across honey-colored vigas like a woven piece of homespun. The floor was hardened and polished dried mud. The room was a generous-sized rectangle with a small cubicle in one corner which contained a hole in its floor big enough to hold a standing man: what for, I had no idea.

There was the door we came through and one small window. To our right was a bare, square room with one window and a beautiful corner fireplace with a raised hearth. To the left was the main meeting room: its floor a step lower than the first two rooms, which made the ceiling higher.

On one of the vigas was painted the date this particular Brotherhood chapter was organized, the date the building was erected, and the date it was dedicated, all in 1934.

At the end below the bell tower was a simple main entrance door of narrow planks, and right in the middle and to the front of the room was a wood heating stove. At the far end, where the altar had been, was a raised plank floor and a rounded end wall. The adobe walls in this room were covered with wallpaper. On the west wall were three of the small square windows.

My companion held one end of a tape measure while I measured the place from the inside. Then he did a watercolor of the outside while I stayed inside to get the feel of the place. When he took me to the train for Chicago, he handed me a large pad, pencil and eraser, and said: "You're going to need these."

There was a fierce blizzard, and the train got to Garden City and sat there for sixteen hours without moving. In that sixteen hours I drew a plan for the morada—made sketches of the interior, of cabinets that I would make, and bancos—the whole picture. When I showed them to the Bennetts in Chicago, they asked, "How soon can you get started?"

I started in April, 1954. The first thing I had to do was find a place to live in Taos. Mrs. Bennett got me a studio at the Harwood Foundation until the first of June, at which time a student of the Foundation would arrive. There were several of these studios for students which all had temporary people in them otherwise.

Mine, a main room, kitchen, and bath, was the first one to the left by the main entrance, just past Ernest Blumenschein's house a few doors back. On the other side of the Foundation was Emil Bisttrams' studio house. They had been our guests at the Houston artist's gallery Sted and I had belonged to, and he was very complimentary about the oils I was showing—but he earned my dislike when he was drumming up summer students for himself by stating, in a talk he gave at the Houston Art Museum, that Houston had no real artists. Several of our artists signed up with him to become "real," but not me.

The Harwood was generously supported by Mrs. Wurlitzer of the Wurlitzer Piano Company. She provided scholarships for many of the artists she felt worthy. She lived in Taos and the librarian at the Harwood lived in her house and told me Mrs. Wurlitzer spent most of her days standing at her windows looking out at the mountains.

There was a wonderful collection of art in the Harwood Gallery, by the original ten called the Taos Society of Artists. The group included Joseph Sharp, E. Irving Couse, Ernest Blumenschein, Oscar Berninghaus, Bert Phillips, Herbert Dunton, Walter Ufer, Victor Higgins, Catherine Critcher and Kenneth Adams. But the show also included collections from later arrivals to the Taos colony. This is a permanent collection and I have seen it many times.

An undirected sketch class met once a week and I attended it, meeting some of the newer arrivals as well as the older ones. I was fascinated by one who made luscious nude drawings with a dip pen and bottle of ink. He smeared the ink with his fingers where he wanted shading. The pen is one of the most demanding tools an artist can use, but when used deftly gives the most expressive use of the person's hand and thought. I am more devoted to the pen, I think, than the brush...how can I say that? I love it all.

Margo got me an Indian crew from Taos Pueblo, two women and two men from the John D. Concha family and one uncle and his daughter. They were perfect. They knew just where to get good adobes and stones and who to see to get timbers and how to do the work I needed. The women did the plastering of the walls and filled the cracks between the small aspen saplings in the ceiling so dirt wouldn't fall through. The men opened windows in walls where there had been none, built the few inner and outer walls I needed, and did the cement work and carpentry.

I put out the word that I needed old handmade doors. Neighbors showed up with a four-inch key to a door they had; when I went to see the door I bought it, as well as a two-foot deep door casing and an old table. They gave me an old hanging gas lamp, too.

In the village of Trampas I found a lady who was remodeling her grandfather's house. She was taking out all the old doors and handmade hanging shelves and handmade Rio Grande rugs, and was replacing them with stock doors and linoleum.

One night after work my old collie dog and I went up to her house in a storm. I stayed all night and helped her pit a washtub of cherries and slept on a high stack of Rio Grande handwoven rugs stashed under her mattress, my dog by the bedside. The next morning I took a screwdriver and removed the bedroom door where I had slept. She promised to ask her husband, who was out herding sheep, if I could buy another door I'd found, one he had salvaged for his goat house. A few weeks later I saw her in a Taos dime store and she told me her husband would sell me the door. Both were heavy, with hand-grooved paneling and put together with dowels.

In the morada I found a beautiful latch that hooked into a simple catch. I took it back to Santa Fe, to Mr. Apodaca, a blacksmith who lived on Apodaca Hill, off Canyon Road. He made me a barrel of those latches, as well as other pieces of iron I asked him to do.

"How do I get them to look old?" I wanted to know.

He took care of that by burying them at the foot of a post where the dog came to piddle. I got them a few weeks later, and you couldn't tell them from the original.

One of the most prominent figures in the cultural life of Taos was Frank Waters, the eminent American writer. Many of his books had a mystical tone to them; he felt a protective instinct toward the spiritual traditions of the Taos area. When he heard that I was turning a Penitente morada into a house, he and his wife came charging over on horseback to stop me.

But after they saw what I was doing, they decided it was a beautiful thing, and I never saw them again or heard anything more from them. The local people came and said, "Muy bonita," and brought me homemade bread and invited me to their houses.

We built a fireplace in the rounded and raised area where the altar had been and bancos from the fireplace along the rounded wall. Under the bancos I left a passageway, sealed in for cold air to go to the fireplace and be heated, then let out above. We laid flagstones on the floor in this raised altar area, and in the kitchen and bath; in the rest of the house we just repaired the adobe floors. The look of the outside remained as it was, the bell and tower and cross and simplicity of line. I did add a patio wall and doorway to it.

The only serious incident in the whole venture occurred when we were putting in the plumbing for the kitchen. The Indians digging the trenches ran into a wooden coffin. The whole crew was spooked and it was two weeks before I could get them to come back to the job. We ceremoniously covered the coffin back up and brought the plumbing lines in from the outside. Whenever I spent the night at the morada, which I often did during the remodeling, the Indians would ask me each morning if I'd seen ghosts in the night. I never did but I felt their friendly presence.

All of the cupboards in the bath and kitchen and the bedroom closet doors were made of old gray wood that I had to remove from the board-and-batten pitched roof. A V-Valley galvanized tin roof replaced the old one. I hated to change the roof but had to for practical purposes. The V-Valley gave a similar effect. For my cupboard doors I used the same technique of board for the backing and batten in the front to create decorative panels, as on the old doors I'd found in Trampas.

The place was ready for the Bennetts when they came at the end of summer. I can still hear them exclaiming at this and that as they went through the front entrance to the back bedroom and out into the walled courtyard. He went ahead of her and she followed like a squaw.

Sometimes Benny didn't send the money so I could pay the men, and I would have to use my own. I had gone to his banker to get him to make some arrangement to assure a steady flow. But instead of calling Benny himself, the Taos banker called the Chicago bank and Benny got the message in a roundabout way he didn't like.

He was real hurt, and mad at me. I tried to explain but he wasn't listening. Finally I shouted, "I love you, Benny!"

Well, that stopped him and put a whole new light on the subject, but the money came without any further difficulty. I made sure, one day when we were having lunch together, to tell Eleanor I loved her—in front of him. My love for the morada, and my love for them and the morada, were always one.

The Bennetts were patrons of the arts; when they were in town it was a sociable time. They wanted me with them in everything they were doing. I saw friends and met people I otherwise wouldn't have met. Everywhere I went, it was the houses I was interested in more than the people—yet it was the people who made the houses.

Painter Howard Cook and his wife Barbara Latham I give as an example: I have only a hazy recollection of what he looked like and not the vaguest notion of what she looked like. But I know they had the most beautiful adobe floors! They were highly polished and I could see straw below the polish, rich and golden. There were Indian rugs and hand-carved Taos beds for sofas. I remember flowers, and Howard's rhythmic and mystical paintings in earth colors. I remember Barbara's realistic watercolors—one of a burial ground at a church, with white carved grave-crosses with artificial flowers hanging on them.

I finally met Ernest Blumenschein's daughter, Helen. She came by the morada one day to bring the Bennetts her two books, "Sounds and Sights of Taos Valley" and "Petroglyphs in Rio Arriba County." She was dressed for pick-and-shovel work and was headed out to dig out a buried ancient Indian pit house. Her dog was with her. She simply left the books and departed.

Every once in a while I see a Taos artist or a writer and they tell me: "I met you at the Bennett morada when the Bennetts gave a party in your honor." They not only remember me, but they remember the morada, in detail, as a work of beauty.

The city of Taos is one thing—but to be able to go into its adobe homes and gardens is a richer and more rewarding experience than one can imagine (the same is true of Santa Fe).

I like inviting people to see my house. That is hardly true of every artist or writer (and not true of me when I'm busy.) Mary Austin, a Santa Fe writer of the 1920s and 30s, was so bothered when people just walked in on her that she'd as soon turn the garden hose on them as not.

The Bennetts wrote notes and developed correspondences that lasted a lifetime. I have some wonderful letters from them, and from their sons. Benny died in the morada a few years later and Eleanor died a year or two after that, but one son and his bride had me go with them to the morada for their honeymoon.

When I was a guest at the morada I slept on a banco in the living room and fell asleep watching the firelight flicker on the beams and latia ceiling, listening to the quiet.

CHAPTER 21

Every year, there were orchards to prune, ditches to clean, houses to redecorate, hot water heaters to come and go, pumps in wells to be repaired or replaced. And there were illustrations to do for New Mexico Magazine. One of these was of a little boy who went to the cathedral and lifted the Christ child out of his manger (under the Virgin Mother's benevolent eyes) to give him a ride around the plaza in a little red wagon. This was to fulfill a promise he'd made when he had prayed for a wagon for Christmas and got it.

My father died on Christmas Eve in 1958. He was in the patio that afternoon, talking with Wilfred and Edith, my new daughter-in-law, who was also a medical student. As I was doing some last-minute shopping at Kaune's Grocery Store, I was paged. Wilfred wanted to tell me that my father was having trouble breathing and he thought we should get him to the hospital.

Study and work we had been doing had been very important. Now I knew he was ready to go. He died just before midnight. When we left the hospital, we were immediately reminded that it was Christmas—time for the Christ to be born.

All the buildings in Santa Fe were outlined with luminarios on their wall-top copings. Luminarios are grocery-bag sacks turned down at the top to make them firm, and filled with two or three inches of sand which holds a lighted candle in place. They were arranged a few feet apart. It's an old custom.

We drove in silence, taking in this magic, along with the magic of life and death that we felt that night.

One morning, a short while afterwards, I was going out to my car to go to town. An Indian, coming down my drive, called out to me:

"There's a rattlesnake here in the road. Shoot it!"

"There's a hoe hanging on the fence right there. You kill it!"

"Indians don't kill snakes. You shoot it."

So I put my things down, went back to the house, got my gun, and shot the snake in two.

"Me and my dog were just looking for my old white horse," and he left.

It was years before I saw an Indian on my place after that. I had been worried about letting them know that my dad was gone. Not because they were hostile. On the contrary, I was afraid one might think I needed a man on the place.

I was reminded of something that someone—Mabel Dodge Lujan, Alice Corbin Henderson, or maybe Mary Austin—had written. Whoever it was had been invited to spend the night in an Indian Pueblo house so she could be there to see an early morning Indian dance performance. She slept on the floor with an Indian man rolled up in a blanket on either side of her for her protection. Their idea, not hers.

The two houses I remodeled that year for Carrel and Bill had been built of adobe by Fred Hoen, the man who ran the nursery for Gene and Louise Callin, the former owners of both our Cottonwood ranch and the Williams' ranch.

In 1932, the highway had come through the middle of the Callin Ranch; the houses were only about thirty and forty feet from the edge of the road. Both of them were functional but unattractive. Fred had built the smaller one for a filling station and sandwich shop; the larger one was in an L-shape and, when I first saw it in 1932, there were just outside walls with a pitched roof overhead.

The inside had been cut up with inside partitions into small rooms and awkward hallways. I knew the roof wouldn't fall in, so I took out some of those partitions and opened it up. And I gave the adobe some character by softening its hard lines. The filling station was only a few steps back from the L-shaped house; both buildings sat on the bank of an arroyo. There was a grassy beach before the deep part of the arroyo and a lot of very old cottonwoods.

The filling station was crude, with a frame room at one end; it, too, was cut up into small rooms. I tore down the tacked on frame room, tore out stud partitions and built soft adobe buttresses to the front opening and transformed the whole place.

I had gotten furniture from Carrel and Bill's other house and I had the little place ready for them to spend a month in. I had laid a fire in the big fireplace in the living room for the cool of the evenings; curtains up and everything. And I had the other house rented.

I drained my savings that year with all the pressure tanks I had to buy for wells, septic tank fields I had to relay, plastering that had to be done and fruit to pick and cars to fix.

But I looked at the beauty around me and the mountain and I said, "Oh God, you have been good to me, with all this beauty."

Then I looked at the mountains again and said: "Go away, I can't eat you!"

Then I turned to God and yelled, "Help!"

Meanwhile, Carrel and some other neighbors had told me a year ago about some people who wanted me to do some remodeling and build an addition to their house. I'd forgotten about them because I'd heard they had inherited a lot of money. I'd thought, "Some high-powered architect will get a hold of that." So when it turned up again, I figured it was because I'd yelled for help.

The neighbors came and got me and took me bodily up to Pojoaque to meet the Caprons. I took one look at the house and recognized it as a house built right out of the book Sted had done on Santa Fe homes in 1936 (a house I'd remodeled for Irene Peck in Santa Fe had also been built from that book).

I knew I was hooked, this was my job. I looked around and saw marvelous possibilities for the large living room, library, bedroom and bath to be added to the house. The house was sitting above a river with huge cottonwoods and a barranca, or bluff, on the other side of the river.

I measured and made a sketch of the floor plan and went home. The next morning I called the Caprons and told them I had a plan I'd like to show them. Mrs. Capron said, "There's a ditch-digger finishing a job in the neighborhood this morning. Can we get him over to start the foundations?"

The foundations were dug. There was no contract, no time for getting blueprints. The Caprons set up a joint account in my name and theirs. A crew was assembled, adobes purchased and delivered—vigas, flagstones, everything. Once, all I needed was a piece of baling wire and it turned up at my feet. I was continually, quietly, saying "Thanks, God."

My new living room was thirty-eight feet long and seventeen feet wide, with large windows that looked up and down the river. One whole end we shelved for the library. There was a door leading into our new twenty-by-sixteen foot bedroom, and a door from that into the new patio and another to the new bath.

We installed another (double) door which led out of the living room onto our new fifty-two-foot portal above a pond where otters could be seen tunneling through the water on a quiet day.

My walls for the new living room were two-foot-thick adobe. The new ceiling had large round vigas with peeled aspen latias for decking. For the floor we used flagstones and we built a fireplace in the living room and bedroom.

After we'd moved the furniture in, a blind man came to tune the piano. He was led by his small daughter. As they came in through the big door off the portal he stopped and stood still. We all looked up and had shivers roll down our spines when he said, "This is a beautiful room."

At one point someone from the county came to inspect the job. I could tell that he came in a skeptical and militant mood, but in no time at all his mood completely changed. He was so complimentary when he left that I thought he was going to kiss my hand.

I always wore a blue-jean skirt and big silver bracelet. There were no glasses or thick mannish shoes—just a woman, five-foot-two, straight black hair parted in the middle, drawn and pinned into a chignon, sun-tanned high cheekbones, dark-eyed and sandal-footed. One friend had commented to another that "you might find Myrtle on the roof or under the sink, but you'll never find her in blue-jean pants."

After I had the new part finished, we cut a wide opening through to the old part. I changed a bedroom into a kitchen and the old kitchen into a bedroom. When we cut the opening from the old part to the new, we found there was already a lintel in the wall for an opening.

During the course of the work I learned that an architect had made an elaborate modern house plan for the Caprons which they had turned down. With my plan and the remodeling we did, we had a beautiful and truly functional house. But the neighbors got lost in it during the opening party because it was so changed.

The Caprons lived in the old part the while we were working and every time I passed the kitchen door they had coffee for me. I would say, "Just an inch."

If I needed adobes, Rody Capron took me to see some somewhere in his Jaguar, and kept telling me I needed a little sports car. I had a station wagon—it was my car, truck and studio. I never thought I could do without it but when Rody brought in a little long English Racing Triumph 4, in gray and black with a white soft top, I traded what he still owed me for it.

The day I traded for the sports car, Wilfred called and said, "You know what Edith and I were thinking? We were thinking that you should buy yourself a smaller car and give us the station wagon." They had three growing children, a girl and two boys.

So I took them the station wagon and drove home with their ailing Studebaker. The thing had a gasoline leak under the hood, but I got home and got a hundred and fifty dollars for it.

That car had always been a disaster. While Wilfred was still at the university he'd called me one night while I was having a party and he asked if he could have a couple of hundred dollars. He wanted to trade his little red jeep for this newly-painted, robin's-egg blue Studebaker.

I asked, "What's the matter with your jeep?"

He said, "Well, the girls get their dresses spoiled riding in it."

I told him I'd send the money. Then I got my broom and, in the middle of the party, started sweeping up crumbs on the floor.

Someone said, "Myrtle always gets her broom out and starts sweeping when she's disturbed about something."

Both Wilfred and Tom—and in fact their wives and all the children—always have ended their telephone conversations with "We love you, Mom" or "We love you, Grandma." They've always been my greatest admirers and greatest companions as well as my standby critics.

CHAPTER 22

Once I drove my little car to New York, parked it on twentieth Street, and then looked down on it from fourteen stories up. And at night I often looked up from the car at the sky on Wall Street and out at the boats along the dock. By day I took a taxi and went to galleries, and to publishing houses. Once, I left this book in manuscript form in a cab. While I was studying jewelry in a show window, the taxi went around the block and then came back with my manuscript. I hadn't missed it but I challenge anyone who says New York is an unfriendly place.

All the way, going and coming home, I had to unlock the hood of my Triumph with a big key (which looked like the water company key) for garage people and show them where everything was. Most of them had never seen such a car. If I'd needed a part somewhere, I'd be sitting there yet.

Wilfred and Edith were finishing their medical training and planning to practice in Santa Fe. In expectation of their return, I had asked a doctor and his family who'd been in the Big House for twelve years to move so I could get the house ready for them.

But instead of coming to Santa Fe, Wilfred and Edith stayed in Denver and he developed a good practice as an orthopedic surgeon; Edith as an anesthesiologist. They bought a beautiful house with a swimming pool and a view of the city and the mountains and later a mountain retreat west of Denver.

So I shuttled back and forth to Denver and also to Washington D.C. where Marion and Tom and their three girls had gone so that Tom could attend Washington University for special training that the Air Force wanted him to have. He was stationed at the Pentagon after his training at Washington University. They bought a home in McLean, Virginia.

These trips gave me a chance to see a completely different environment. I enjoyed the museums as well as the family life and often got a trip as a Christmas gift from Tom and Marion or Wilfred and Edith.

I rented my own house to an opera composer one summer, then to a couple of doctors and their families. The second summer Dora, a friend who lived in the first William's house that I built across the street from me, went to Wood's Hole and I stayed in her house. She was worried about her two sons who were coming back home with her.

"Isn't there something we can fix up for Peter?" she'd been asking me. "He and Charles don't get along in the same room."

Outside her house, a few feet away, was an adobe chicken house. Dora was renting her house from the Williams'; I was in charge. Bill had told me: "Do anything you want with the place, Myrtle. I have full confidence. You don't even have to ask."

So I used my own money in compensation for staying at Dora's and turned the eight-by-twelve foot chicken-house into a room for Peter. It had a large window opening on the sunny side, with plastic over it. I put in a window, built a tiny fireplace in one corner, plastered the walls and laid a flagstone floor. I put some decoration on the plank door that made it thicker and good-looking.

While I was working on one of Bill's houses, I got Big Joe's Lumber Company in Santa Fe to replace two narrow long glass panels with rounded tops in the upper part of an old Colonial door for me. One of the men was carrying the door through the store and toward my car when he passed a tall, gaunt figure in black boots, black pants, black five-eighths-length coat and a black turban.

She stretched her arm out at full length and pointed a long, black-gloved finger.

She said, "I want that door."

I said, "Sorry, Georgia O'Keeffe; you can't have this door, but if I ever see another one I'll let you know."

She said, "I know who you are," and I thought to myself that even her words sounded black, but I was pleased that she knew me.

Santa Fe didn't have many doctors when Sted and I first came, but high in altitude, it seemed close to the Great Physician. When the late evening sun tinged the Sangre de Cristo Mountains, you could imagine a priest naming the effect "The Blood of Christ."

Ruled for a hundred and fifty years by the crown of Spain and the cross of the Catholic Church, impregnated with the beat of Indian drums, shot up with arrows and by the guns of the U.S. Militia and the desperadoes, Santa Fe remained as unperturbed as the earth from which it rose.

Cupped by three mountain ridges, a river of life running through it with stately poplars and ancient cottonwoods marking its path and watershed, Santa Fe is a Governor's Palace, a place populated by people who work for the state, people who were born here, people who came here to live, people who came here to paint or write, people who just came to look.

There are so many artists and writers here that we are prone to look at the landscape as a Maxfield Parrish, a Dole Reed, an Ernest Blumenschein, or through the eyes of our favorite poets—and every adobe house might look like a Myrtle or Wilfred Stedman house.

Santa Fe is well aware of its special qualities—even now we haggle and politic to keep it in line. Yet a description of that line would be in the nature of a paradox, of sharp contrasts holding together a homogeneous mass, of an ethereal substance—of ancient unquestioning ceremony hand in hand with explosive ideas, of brilliant light and deepest shadows, red earth against blue, blue sky. All around are the evidences of dried-up sea beds basking in the sun, dotted with pinon and domed by sky. The most ancient cliff dwellings and adobe structures exhibit an extensive use of solar technology.

In the summertime, in the 1960s, I was working on Wilfred and Edith's summer retreat, and later in the 1970s and 1980s, I rented my house to the Santa Fe Opera. The first two summers, director John Crosby rented it; then directors, composers and visiting dignitaries of the opera world. Sometimes I'd be in one of my other studio houses working on a book or painting, and was around to join my guests in endless early dinner parties on the patio. Or I would cook up a pot of posole for everyone.

Jim Dixon, who was Crosby's assistant director for two seasons, stayed on into the winter one year after the opera season was over. He took my studio and I moved back into the house. He was writing and we spent an occasional tea-time or dinnertime talking about our work.

Stephen Wadsworth of the Metropolitan Opera was working on the opera, "A Quiet Place," with Leonard Bernstein in my house one summer. Stephen was a delight but I only knew most of the opera people by the notes they left me. I was away while Leonard Bernstein was at the house.

My house is not a pretentious one. It hasn't anything in it of irreplaceable value, except a sense of peace and quiet, yet the notes left by visitors tell me it's got to be one of the world's greatest houses. If I asked someone to stay in it for a few days or a couple of weeks, I'd find a poem when I came back, telling me of that certain something about the place that makes even the weeds seem beautiful; a summer flower holding a bit of light or in winter a bit of snow.

The house is just below the Santa Fe Opera. It's a place for birds and wildlife, pastures and paths to walk on. The old cottonwoods lining the river bank and the arroyos at both ends of the place give it a studied naturalness. There is a trimmed and neat look; but a wildness and sheer neglect in the wooded areas.

Inside, there's an eleven-foot table; a bird-feeder on the portal post just outside, and a long view of the mountains beyond. There are lilac bushes, hollyhocks, and turtle doves that have been here longer than the house and there's brilliant sunlight and deep shadow, and high mountain air that sweeps down the foothills and along the valley floor and over the wild white morning-glories that halo the clipped lawn around the house.

My places—the houses—often make people think of Georgia O'Keeffe's house. Both of us have had a way of making a lot out of a little—like building in a three-by-twelve by fourteen foot plank for a shelf across the end of a room, as the walls are going up, on which we might set one Indian pot and nothing else.

I like what she said once, in her writing or in an interview: that if she were to build another house, it would be so simple that it would make all other houses look like Chinese puzzles.

Our adobe houses are like pieces of sculpture—designed to sit on, write on, and live in; ornamented by space. Anything intimate or private—such as a chair or a table strewn with books or papers—looks a hundred percent more intimate or private in such a setting.

I am not nearly as private as Georgia was. Once I took a sculptress to Georgia's place in Abiquiu. She thought she had to see Georgia while she was in New Mexico: it wouldn't be right not to pay homage to so great a fellow artist. Strings were pulled and a great deal of preparation made; finally she got her invitation.

We were met at the gate by two big dogs and Georgia's secretary. I hesitated, but was pulled in by my friend. Inside Georgia's clinically clean studio, I was "assigned" to a chair and told to be seated. My friend was escorted into the next room to see Georgia."

I sat approving the big window, the landscape beyond, and the bed at the window, draped in a crisp white sheet and one puffy down pillow in a white pillowcase. I noticed a bronze plaque on the wall—from Georgia's neighbors, celebrating her generosity to the village. There were two or three watercolors with just a squiggle of paint. I was hardly conscious of the agitated talk going on in the next room. But soon my friend came out, and we were quickly escorted back through the gate.

"Well, Myrtle," she began, "you would never believe what happened."

"I'll bet I would."

I knew Georgia had refused to see Ernest Blumenschin and others—even close friends were assigned to a chair on the far side of the room while Georgia sat and contemplated whatever she was contemplating before she got interrupted; or they received a scolding, as my friend had, and were sent on their way.

Georgia had refused to autograph my friend's copy of her book. "My book is enough," she'd said.

I like Georgia's book, "Georgia O' Keeffe." It is beautifully done. The reproductions of her work are clear and true. I like especially her paintings of New York, and I like the way she wrote about her work. It is enough for me. I feel closer to Georgia than to any other painter, though I can't even say that I knew her.

It was now twenty years since Sted had died, and I began to take stock. I was happy about all my good fortune. But then one day I started to cry and cried for two weeks solid. The main part of my problem was what to do about a pressing social habit of giving part or all of one's estate away to family members while still living, an idea that the law favors tax-wise. My parents had given practically everything they owned away, holding to the notion that their children would in turn take care of them in their latter days. I resisted the idea and also the idea of breaking my property up. It was so perfect as a whole. I counted heavily on the security of having it just as it was, to enjoy myself, and in having the boys and their children enjoy—but as mine for now, and this is what the law also should favor for the solidarity of the family and of the family estate.

I had a medium-sized suitcase of checks I'd written in the past twenty years; I went through them and brought all my records up to date. I settled satisfactory business with the boys about the estate, having to do with Sted's will, and dried my tears.

I had served for five years as a representative from my community at the Pojoaque Watershed District Board meetings, twelve years as a member of the Santa Fe County Recreational Advisory Council, two years as a board member of a tri-community group known as Las Tres Villas— during which time we successfully kept the kids of Tesuque School from being bussed into the consolidated Santa Fe School District (which made news throughout the country.) I had been called upon for "this and that and the other things," as an old woman I knew used to say. Now I was ready to close all the books and call it a day.

I met an English and Drama professor at an art exhibit. I asked him to read "Of One Mind" and give me an opinion of it. He read it and began to demonstrate what he thought about it; he was stirred only in the usual way of understanding the male and female. I had to keep a big chair between us while he did a few snatchings at me; finally he went out through the kitchen and took the bottle of wine he had brought.

I was a mean woman to all who would have taken me by force; I admired none, except as a friend or professional. But when one I had loved (along with his wife) for years appeared at my door for a lonely visit while his wife was away, it was something else. He had called and asked if he could come and I'd said, "Of course." But something in his voice made me apprehensive. His wife often made a joke about how he "couldn't do it anymore."

Because of his meticulous care in dress and the eagerness in the usual kiss he gave me at the door, I wasn't at all surprised when he started to strip me right in the doorway. I managed to get us both out the door and onto the porch, but saw immediately that that was a mistake, so I let him in.

An artist contemplates his naked canvas before him, a poet his paper, an archer draws his bow. They may all plunge in to do the work at hand, but only when the canvas, paper and bow are in a receptive attitude can the expression assert itself to resemble a creative accomplishment.

I invited another old friend and his wife to come to dinner.

"My wife's not with me anymore," he said. (He was an architect.)

"Oh, well, come on out by yourself."

"All right, I'll do that."

I wanted to show him the illustrations for a new book I was working on. I looked forward to an inspiring, invigorating intellectual evening, but he became distracted by a split skirt I was wearing.

"Can't you put on a robe? That thing's too tight."

I took him by the hand and led him to the bedroom and showed him where he could hang his clothes. That seemed to scare him out of his wits for the rest of the evening. When I sent him off, he backed out of the house repeating, "You lied to me when you told me you were seventy years old."

Sex, I always figured, was a way of communicating, an intercourse helping us to realize mind and body are one—the bread and wine if you will—or if you won't, it's all the same to me.

CHAPTER 23

I know.

Light is the brilliance of Mind—darkness gives it depth and form...

In the beginning, darkness slept—but, dreaming of light, grew restless. So light appeared, inspiring the virgin concept.

Where there is an emptiness, there is a filling—it is as simple as that!

This is what love is—a satisfactory giving and taking. No reason is involved.

Yet in this very act is life and creativity, the God power within.

This is what makes life passionate and endearing. This I have experienced.

———

I also experienced the death of a grandson; he shot himself. I almost lost Wilfred, too, from a heart attack brought on by trying to cope with the boy and with his high-tension orthopedic surgery practice at the same time.

The boy was seventeen; he dreamed of being a writer, but was quietly at odds with himself, his school and the world. In the eight summers I spent in the mountains he, more than any other member of the family, was with me—helping me to work on the houses, making me go fishing with him, reading and talking together. He loved my book; he said, "Grandma, you should write poetry."

I did, after he was gone, to save my own sanity—deep and heart-rending lines.

We almost lost Tom's wife—actress and play director—that same year. After 23 years, Tom retired from the Air Force and organized his own home improvement business in the Washington area doing beautiful work remodeling houses. Wilfred and Edith left the medical practice; Edith to a literary interest and Wilfred to sculptoring and painting, with good galleries handling his work, and teaching medical anatomy to artist and sculpture students in art schools and workshops, at the Ringling Brothers in Sarasota, Florida and the Scottsdale Artists School in Arizona.

In the winter, for long stretches of time, I lived like a monk in retreat on my ranch, for weeks on end seeing no one—painting, writing, reading and watching the snow fall. Then, all of a sudden, my house would be like Grand Central Station with family, friends or others.

I designed and built other houses and consulted with people about adobe architecture; wrote and illustrated four books on that subject, based on forty years' experience and "Of One Mind" was published.

And I entered into a real pleasant place in the sun with Alice Bullock, author of "Living Legends of the Santa Fe Country;" with Peggy Pond Church, author of "The House at Otowi Bridge;" and other writers of the day.

I renewed my acquaintance with Helen Blumenschein which had been rich and rewarding. Helen and I used to go painting together, but usually our conversations turned to leaky roofs and fallen-down portals.

About this time, one of my paintings was selected for the permanent collection of the New Mexico Museum of Fine Arts and I prepared a memorial exhibition of Sted's work for the same museum. I put together photo albums of my adobe houses and filled six three-inch albums with chronological scrapbook material of our work which was microfilmed for the Smithsonian.

I succeeded, after years of struggle, in getting the Santa Fe school system to let me re-design the Tesuque School playground and parking area under a grant which made the school more serviceable as a recreational and educational meeting-place for the whole community. I officiated in the dedication program.

I had long been a member of the Old Santa Fe Association, which was organized in the 1920s to keep an eye on the growth of Santa Fe—to keep the town in line with its traditions and style of Southwestern architecture. Nothing pleases me more than the sight of Santa Fe when I arrive home after having been away.

I belonged to the San Gabriel Historical Society, the Colonial New Mexico Historical Foundation and the St. Vincent's Hospital Auxiliary and painted six murals for the hospital. I became a member of the St. John's Library Association, never missing a book-and-author lecture or luncheon. I am classified as an "Angel" Guild member of the Santa Fe Opera. In fact, the forest of deciduous trees at the Opera all came from my place, simply as a response to director John Crosby's asking.

Once I was especially invited to an Old Santa Fe Association board meeting at architect John Gaw Meem's house. The purpose, unbeknownst to me, was to discuss a proposal to sell the old downtown Santa Fe High School site to Montgomery Ward. When the proposal was made I waited for a second before I broke the lull by stating that, since the site already belonged to the city, it should be used for a city municipal complex. At that time, the municipal offices were scattered all over town, mostly in old converted homes. I think I was one of only two women there and I was the only one who spoke. I saw eyebrows go up all around the circle of men and it was unanimously voted that this would be our proposal to the city. And this is what was eventually done.

My voice was spoken of as a ball of fire following a meeting at the St. Francis Auditorium, where the discussion was a debate as to whether Santa Fe should have a historic zone. And we got the historic zone.

I went about all these things as though they were of the utmost importance—as though I were doing them for someone else. The more I could identify myself with the "other self" of the Mind, the more I could do. I saw three of Sted's paintings go to museum collections and some illustrations to the Rice Institute Archives in Houston. I had three art shows, and I did something I'd always wanted to do by going to the New York Art Students' League to study with four important painters in 1979.

And now it is 1989, and I am ahead with four grandsons-in-law, seven great-grand children and am seriously thinking I'll soon have a one-and-only grand-daughter-in-law.

It is no wonder Sted seems to hold himself aloof when I dream of him. He used to tell me: "I don't know what sustains you."

I've been honored by "Santa Fe Network for the Common Good" as a Santa Fe "Living Treasure" (one who serves as an inspiration for many in the celebration of the human spirit). I've been photographed and written up. What can I say?

After a busy day I take my dog and we walk out the path to the lower orchard where it's cool—with the evening light coming down in long shafts off the bluff above the river, glistening on every leaf and blade of grass. At length we climb to a higher level where the cottonwoods are tall, young and old, and I sit on a log looking down upon the river.

And I hear Sted's proverbial question: "What took you so long to get home?" Now, I answered, "I've been sharing all the things that you inadvertently taught me—and more."

And I think of the lines from "Of One Mind":

This is an ideal universe, governed by what is uppermost in the mind. Fortunately, this is the mind's own consciousness of itself.

The light shineth in the darkness...but it should not be said anymore...and the darkness comprehended it not (John 1:5).

The darkness is the evidence of the receptive nature of the mind.

When I saw the dark abyss, I asked What is the abyss? And I heard "Open mind" and the abyss was promptly filled with light.

The open mind is the womb that gives form to that which it has come to know, and is the means of satisfying its own longings.

To know and be known of the mind is wisdom and understanding.

In view of this light, the virgin darkness of the mind has lost none of its purity.

She was always, and is ever, the bride.

And he, the light, her bridegroom.

Our own identity can be placed with one or the other and then both, in the full consciousness of Being.

Mind discloses its own immaculate conception of itself in love.

In love we bear witness to its Love.

═══════

   My love for Tom makes me see his dark eyes—makes me hear him say, "Hi Mom." Two years ago we lost him to cancer.

   I had told him, "I know you are not deliberately preparing a new environment for yourself but this is what I feel you are doing. It is probably the equivalent to the thousand acre dream you had but never realized. Or you are getting ready to have a part of this place when I am through with it though that would be a compromise Tom, in comparison to your own dream—it's not too late for whatever."

   My thoughts turn to my mother and to our first serious discussion about God and about Sted. "Mama, someday I am going to write a wonderful poem about you. You gave me so much of your sense of the spiritual nature of all things, though I gave you a bad time in the way I perceived that sense, but I was so right in the way I felt about Sted and still do."

   I looked out and beyond the river and closed my eyes. An image of a door caught my attention. Its whole center became an oval of light and I stepped through and there was Sted. Neither of us said a word as I walked up to him and put my arms around him.

   My eyes opened and I cried for an hour and a half with the deepest sobs of joy I have ever known.

END